saur

INTERNATIONAL COUNCIL
ON ARCHIVES

CONSEIL INTERNATIONAL
DES ARCHIVES

ICA Handbooks Series
Volume 3

Dictionary
of Archival Terminology

Dictionnaire
de terminologie archivistique

English and French
With Equivalents in Dutch, German,
Italian, Russian and Spanish

Edited by Peter Walne
Compiled by Frank B. Evans, François-J. Himly
and Peter Walne

K·G·Saur München · New York · London · Paris 1984

CIP-Kurztitelaufnahme der Deutschen Bibliothek

Evans, Frank B.:
Dictionary of archival terminology : English and French ;
with equivalents in Dutch, German, Italian, Russian
and Spanish = Dictionnaire de terminologie archi-
vistique / comp. by Frank B. Evans, François-J. Himly
and Peter Walne. – München ; New York ; London ; Paris : Saur, 1984.
  (ICA handbooks series ; Vol. 3)
  ISBN 3-598-20275-X
NE: Himly, François-J.: ; Walne, Peter: ; International
Council on Archives: ICA handbooks series ; HST

Photo composition by SatzStudio Pfeifer, Germering bei München
Printed by Weihert-Druck, Darmstadt
Bound by Buchbinderei Kränkl, Heppenheim/Bergstraße

ISBN 3-598-20275-x

Contents / Table des matières

Dictionary of Archival Terminology/Dictionnaire de terminologie archivistique

Indices

Introduction

This *Dictionary of Archival Terminology* is the outcome of the deliberations of a Working Party of the International Council on Archives established in 1977. The members were: — Mr Peter Walne (United Kingdom) Chairman, Mr François-J. Himly and Mr Michel Duchein (France), Dr Eckhart G. Franz (Federal Republic of Germany), the late Mr Antonio Arago (Spain), Dr Frank B. Evans (United States of America and official Unesco representative), Mr Filip J. Dolgih (USSR) and Dr Charles Kecske-méti (Executive Secretary, ICA). The Working Party has had the benefit of discussions and correspondence with many archivists in the course of its work and to them for their helpful comments it is extremely grateful.

The work of compilation was begun with financial assistance from Unesco within its transfer of information and normative programmes and the International Council on Archives expresses its gratitude to Unesco for its support.

This present work is intended to supersede the *Lexicon of Archival Terminology* (Elsevier, 1964), which was itself the result of the work of a Committee on Terminology of the International Council on Archives, which sat from 1954 to 1963. This *Lexicon* was the first attempt on an international scale to draw up a glossary of the main terms then current in archival usage principally in European countries. It was produced in a period of change in the archival world when microforms were in their infancy, when records management was not yet an inseparable component of the archivist's task and when the application of the computer to the production of the archivist's stock-in-trade and to his techniques and practices barely thought of. Now, twenty years on, the archivist's task, his holdings, techniques and practices — and his terminology — have all passed well beyond the classical frontiers of his immediate predecessors.

This *Dictionary* attempts to assemble some 500 definitions of terms in common use throughout the archival profession. It makes no attempt at completeness in every field of archival work nor in either of the two working languages. This would be a task of very considerable difficulty since so much of the archivist's terminology springs from legal necessity and administrative practices, which vary considerably from country to country even within those groups of countries having common legal and administrative backgrounds and traditions, but also because the archivist has traditionally borrowed terminology, both specialised and general from other disciplines. Unlike the librarian and the information scientist, the archivist has less uniformity both in terms and their usage as between one country and another, as between one legal and administrative tradition and another, or even within one country. Thus no dictionary of archival terms can present as neat, comprehensive, uniform and even logical a picture and pattern as can its sister professions.

This volume, therefore, presents the core of concepts common to several languages. The Working Party has, particularly in the case of some of the most basic terms such as *archives* and *records,* drawn up definitions in what it considers to be a sufficiently general and broad outline to include the essential elements in varying national legally enacted definitions. In other cases, such as microforms and computer applications, it has arrived at similar standardised definitions.

The text is arranged in English language alphabetical order of terms with definitions in English, using British conventions of spelling. This is followed by the French equivalent of the term and its French definition, which may not, for reasons of

7

legal and administrative differences between the two traditions, be an exact translation of the English term and definition. Where there is no equivalent term in French archival usage, the English definition is translated directly into French and enclosed in square brackets. Finally, the equivalent terms (without definition) in Dutch, German, Italian, Russian and Spanish are given. In the case of equivalents in languages other than English, users will note that some terms appear in square brackets, an indication that whilst an equivalent word exists in other languages, it is not yet widely used within the archive profession. A blank entry in the equivalent section indicates that no equivalent term exists.

A serial numeration has been given to terms defined in the English language but *not* to entries serving as cross-references only. In this way, users in any of the other six languages may, by using the appropriate language alphabetical indexes which are tied to this serial numeration, locate a term and its definition in the English and French texts. English language cross-references will be found in the appropriate alphabetical place. French cross-references include the appropriate serial number to direct users immediately to the equivalent definition of a term defined in English and then in French without need to refer to the French alphabetical index.

In both English and French language definitions, words italicised indicate terms defined elsewhere in the text. In the case of English, these will be found in their appropriate alphabetical place. In the case of French, however, it will be necessary for the user to refer to the French alphabetical index in order to discover the appropriate serial numerical reference to the English term which is the equivalent of the italicised French word and so arrive at the appropriate definition(s).

In definitions in English, the use of (UK), (US), (Canada) or (Australia) after any particular definition indicates that the usage is confined to the country indicated; otherwise it should be understood that the definition is in general use. A similar distinction is drawn between French, French-Canadian and Belgian usage, between Spanish and Latin American usage and between German usage in the Federal and Democratic Republics and Austria.

Conscious of the limitations of the volume, its compilers hope that it may prove of use to archivists in every country to increase mutual comprehension of each other's usages and practices and that it may, in some measure, serve as model for and stimulate the publication of national glossaries in whatsoever language to assist archivists within any one country to understand better their own archives and their tasks. They also earnestly hope that their work has gone some further way along the road to dispelling 'the present confusion of terms', which the late T R Schellenberg in his book *The Management of Archives* (1965) so aptly said 'is simply the outward expression of an inward confusion of methods'.

This dictionary is also intended to help bridge the gap which continues to exist between archivists and records managers and their colleagues in the field of information science.

Finally, it is hoped that this work will help fill a long-standing need amongst the basic tools for the training and education of archivists and records managers and may also prove of value to users of records and archives.

The Chairman of the Working Party served as its secretary and as general editor of the glossary. To his colleagues on the Working Party and to those other correspondents who have helped in the stimulating work of compilation, he wishes to record his warmest thanks for their help, encouragement and sustenance.

The French text and index are the work of Mr Himly; the German equivalents and index that of Dr Franz; the Russian equivalents and index that of Mr Dolgih and the Spanish equivalents and index that of the late Mr Arago and Mrs Concepción Contel Barea. The Dutch equivalents and index were provided by Dr Eric Ketelaar and the Italian by Dr Elio Lodolini. These last two contributions were added after completion of the work of compilation.

Introduction

Le présent *Dictionnaire de terminologie archivistique* est l'oeuvre d'un groupe de travail établi par le Conseil International des Archives en 1977. Ce groupe était composé de: MM. Peter Walne (Royaume Uni), François-J. Himly et Michel Duchein (France), Eckhart G. Franz (République Fédérale d'Allemagne), le regretté Antonio Arago (Espagne), MM. Frank B. Evans (USA, représentant de l'Unesco), F.I. Dolgih (URSS) et Charles Kecskeméti (Secrétaire exécutif, CIA). Tout au long de son activité, le groupe de travail a pu bénéficier de l'avis de nombreux archivistes, au moyen de discussions et de correspondances; qu'ils acceptent le témoignage de notre reconnaissance.

La compilation a commencé avec le concours financier de l'Unesco au titre du programme de transfert de l'information et de la normalisation, pour lequel le Conseil International des Archives exprime sa sincère gratitude.

Le présent ouvrage est destiné à remplacer le *Lexicon of Archival Terminology* (Elsevier, 1964) réalisé entre 1954 et 1963 par un Comité de Terminologie du Conseil International des Archives. Ce *Lexicon* avait constitué la première tentative internationale pour réunir dans un glossaire les principaux termes d'utilisation courante, à l'époque, dans les archives et, surtout, dans les archives européennes. Il fut réalisé dans une période de mutation du monde archivistique, alors que le microfilmage était encore dans l'enfance; la gestion de documents ne constituait pas encore une partie intégrante de la fonction archivistique et il n'était guère question de songer à l'application de l'informatique, de ses techniques et de ses pratiques au domaine de l'archivistique. Aujourd'hui, vingt ans après, des tâches de l'archiviste, les documents dont il a la garde, ses techniques et ses méthodes professionnelles, aussi bien que sa terminologie, débordent bien au-delà des frontières classiques qui avaient cerné le travail de ses prédécesseurs immédiats.

Ce *Dictionnaire* présente les définitions de quelque 500 termes d'usage courant dans la profession. Il ne prétend nullement à l'exhaustivité, ni pour ce qui est des divers domaines couverts par le métier d'archiviste, ni en ce qui concerne les deux langues de travail. La tâche eût présenté des difficultés quasi insurmontables du fait que nombre de termes utilisés par l'archiviste dérivent directement du langage juridique et administratif, qui varient considérablement d'un pays à l'autre, même si ceux-ci partagent des traditions légales et administratives communes, et aussi parce que les archivistes ont toujours emprunté des termes à d'autres disciplines. A la différence du bibliothécaire et du spécialiste de l'information, l'archiviste ne peut tabler ni sur l'uniformité des termes, ni sur celle de leur usage, non seulement entre pays différents, mais même à l'intérieur d'un pays, tant la terminologie est liée aux traditions légales et administratives. Aussi, aucun dictionnaire des termes archivistiques ne présentera-t-il une image et une structure aussi nettes, complètes, uniformes et logiques que les ouvrages similaires produits par les professions apparentées.

Ce volume définit les concepts essentiels, communs à plusieurs langues. Le groupe de travail a formulé, notamment pour ce qui est des termes aussi fondamentaux qu'*archives* et *document,* des définitions qu'il estime suffisamment larges pour être compatibles avec les différentes définitions nationales telles qu'elles apparaissent dans les textes légaux. Dans d'autres cas, comme celui du microfilmage ou de l'informatique, il a pu parvenir à des définitions normalisées.

10

Les termes se suivent dans l'ordre alphabétique anglais, avec des définitions en anglais orthographiées conformément aux conventions britanniques. Sont donnés en regard les équivalents français du terme avec leur(s) définition(s) en français qui, en raison des différences légales et administratives entre les deux traditions, ne dérivent pas nécessairement des termes et des définitions en anglais. S'il n'existe pas de terme équivalent dans le vocabulaire archivistique français, la définition anglaise traduite en français est placée entre crochets. Enfin, les équivalents allemand, russes, espagnols, italiens et néerlandais sont donnés, sans définition. Le lecteur notera que certains équivalents dans ces cinq dernières langues sont placés entre crochets. Cela indique que le mot correspondant au terme anglais existe dans la langue en question, mais n'est pas d'usage courant en tant que terme archivistique professionnel. L'absence de tout équivalent signale qu'il n'existe pas de terme approprié dans la langue dont il s'agit.

Les termes retenus comme vedettes sont numérotés dans l'ordre alphabétique anglais (aucun numéro n'ayant été attribué aux termes de renvoi). Les six index alphabétiques allemand, espagnol, français, italien, néeerlandais et russe, qui reprennent la même numérotation, permettent à l'utilisateur de retouver, immédiatement à partir de ces langues, la vedette recherchée avec ses définitions anglaise et française. Les termes de renvoi en langue anglaise figurent à leur place dans l'ordre alphabétique. Le numéro qui figure en regard des termes de renvoi français est celui de la vedette sous laquelle l'utilisateur trouvera les définitions en anglais et en français.

Les mots imprimés en italiques dans les définitions aussi bien anglaises que françaises sont eux-mêmes des vedettes définies ailleurs dans le texte. Pour ce qui est de l'anglais, on se reportera directement à la vedette d'après l'ordre alphabétique. Dans le cas du français, l'utilisateur devra rechercher le numéro de la vedette dans l'index alphabétique français.

Les indications (UK), (US), (Canada) ou (Australie) dans les définitions anglaises signalent que l'utilisation du terme dans cette acception particulière est propre au pays mentionné; autrement, le terme est d'usage général. Des indications similaires signalent les acceptions particulières françaises, franco-canadiennes et belges, espagnoles et latino-américaines de même que celles propres à la République Fédérale d'Allemagne, à la République Démocratique Allemande ou à l'Autriche.

Tout en étant conscients des limites du présent volume, les auteurs espèrent qu'il pourra servir aux archivistes de tous les pays en facilitant la compréhension mutuelle des usages et des pratiques professionnels et en stimulant la publication de glossaires nationaux en toutes langues appelés à aider les archivistes à mieux comprendre l'archivistique de leur propre pays. Ils espèrent que leur travail contribuera à dissiper «la présente confusion des termes» qui n'est, selon l'expression pertinente du regretté T.R. Schellenberg dans son livre *The Management of Archives* (1965), que «le reflet perceptible d'une confusion méthodique dans la discipline elle-même».

Le dictionnaire est également destiné à réduire la distance qui subsite toujours entre les archivistes et leurs collègues dans le domaine des la science de l'information.

Enfin, ce travail devrait constituer un outil de formation en archivistique et en gestion de documents dont on ressent depuis longtemps le besoin, et peut-être sera-t-il profitable aux utilisateurs des archives et des documents.

Le Président du Groupe de Travail remplissait également les fonctions de secrétaire et de rédacteur en chef du glossaire. Il tient à exprimer ici sa reconnaissance chaleureuse à ses collègues du Groupe de Travail, ainsi qu'aux autres correspondants pour les encouragements et l'aide constante qu'ils ont bien voulu lui accorder.

Le texte et l'index français sont l'oeuvre de M. Himly. Les équivalents et l'index allemands sont dus à M. Franz, les équivalents et l'index russes à M. Doligih, les équivalents et l'index espagnols au regretté A. Arago et à Mme Concepciòn Contel Barea, les équivalents et l'index italien à M. Elio Lodolini, et les équivalents et l'index néerlandais à M. Eric Ketelaar. Les deux dernières contributions ont été ajoutées après l'achèvement du travail de compilation.

Dictionary
of Archival Terminology

Dictionnaire
de terminologie archivistique

A – Z

ABBREVIATION

A shortened form of a word standing for the whole, frequently used in *description* for words denoting the physical character or form of a *document* e.g. A for *autograph*, ALS for *autograph letter signed*, L for *letter*.

D Afkorting

G Abkürzung

I Abbreviazione, sigla

ABRÉVIATION 1

Forme abrégée tenant lieu d'un mot, fréquemment utilisé dans les *instruments de recherche*, pour indiquer le caractère physique, la langue ou la forme d'un *document*, par exemple *a* pour *autographe*, *f* pour *français*, *l* pour *lettre*, *p* pour *pièce*.

R Аббревиатура

S Abreviatura

ACCESS

(1) The availability of *records (1)* / *archives (1)* for consultation as a result both of legal authorisation and the existence of *finding aids. See also* CLEARANCE: SECURITY CLASSIFICATION:
(2) In *automatic data processing* the method of placing *data (1)* into and retrieving it from a *memory*.

D (1) Toegankelijkheid (existence of finding aids);
en openbaarheid (legal authorisation)
(2) Toegang

G (1) Benutzbarkeit
(2) Zugriff

I (1) Consultabilità
(2) Accesso

COMMUNICABILITÉ 2

(1) Possibilité de consulter des *documents d'archives (1)* résultant de sa conformité à la réglementation.
Voir aussi (89) ACCÈS PAR DÉROGATION, (418) RESTRICTION DE COMMUNICABILITÉ.
(2) En *traitement automatique des données*, mode d'exploitation d'une *mémoire (2)* grâce auquel les *articles* d'un *fichier* peuvent être présentés ou recueillis dans un ordre indépendant de leur position sur le *support*.

R (1) Доступность архивных документов для использования
(2) Доступ

S (1) Accesibilidad
(2) Acceso

ACCESS DATE

The date at which *records (1)* / *archives (1)* become available for consultation by the general public usually determined by the lapse of a specified number of years.

D [Datum van toegankelijkheid]

G Benutzungsgrenze, Freigabedatum

I Data limite della consultabilità

DATE DE COMMUNICATION 3

Première année suivant l'expiration d'un délai de communication, à partir de laquelle un *document d'archives* est consultable.

R —

S [Fecha inicial de libre consulta]

ACCESSIBILITY *See* ACCESS

ACCESSION
(1) The recording of the formal acceptance into *custody* of an *acquisition*.
(2) an *acquisition* so recorded.
See also ACCRUAL.

D (1) Registratie van een aanwinst
(2) Aanwinst

G (1) Akzessionierung
(2) Akzession, Zugang

I (1) Registrazione dell' accessione
(2) Accessione

ENREGISTREMENT DES ACCROISSEMENTS   4
(1) Inscription sur *registre* valant acceptation officielle et obligation de *conservation* des *accroissements* d'un service d'*archives (2),* accompagné, le cas échéant, par le transfert du titre légal de propriété.
(2) [*Accroissement* ainsi enregistré.]

R (1/2) Процедура приема поступающих в архив документов

S (1/2) Ingreso, entrada de fondos

ACCESSION(S) LIST/REGISTER
A *record* of *acquisitions,* usually in chronological order by date of receipt and giving the title of the *accession*.

D Aanwinstenregister

G Zugangsbuch, Akzessionsjournal

I Registro di entrata

REGISTRE DES ACCROISSEMENTS   5
Registre contenant l'inscription, généralement numérotée dans l'ordre chronologique, des *versements*, des *dépôts* et des *acquisitions*, servant de preuve légale de leur entrée dans un service d'*archives (2).*

R Книга поступлений документов

S Registro de entrada

ACCOUNT
A *document* in which monies or goods received and paid or given out are recorded in order to permit periodic totalisation.

D Rekening

G Rechnung

I Conto

COMPTE/LIVRE DE COMPTE   6
Document énumérant des quantités de monnaies ou d'objets matériels entrés ou sortis permettant une totalisation périodique.

R Книга счетов

S Cuenta

ACCRETION *See* ACCRUAL

ACCRUAL
An *acquisition* usually received in accordance with specified

[Versement complémentaire]   7
Versement reçu conformément aux procédures normales et formant le

16

procedures and additional to
series already held. Also called
accretion (US).

D Aanvulling

G Zugang (zu einem bereits be-
stehenden Bestand)

I Versamento integrativo o
periodico

complément d'un *fonds* déjà pris en
charge par un service d'*archives (2)*
ou par un *centre de préarchivage*.

R [Комплектование открытых
фондов архива. Пополне-
ние комплектующегося
архивпого фонда.]

S Transferencia periódica

ACCUMULATION

Records(1)/archives(1) documen-
ting and generated in the course
of the transaction of affairs of any
kind. Usually characterised as a
'natural' accumulation, in contrast
to a *collection*, which is an
'artificial' accumulation.

D [Organisch gegroeid bestand]

G (Organisch) gewachsener Bestand

I Sedimentazione documentaria

[Accumulation]   8
Formation organique de *fonds* par
le fonctionnement normal des institutions de toute nature, par opposition à la formation artificielle qui
est celle de la *collection*.

R [(1)Накопление документов
учреждением - фондообра-
зователем.]
  (2)Документальный фонд

S Crecimiento orgánico

ACIDITY *See* pH VALUE

ACQUISITION

An addition to the *holdings* of a
records centre/archives (2), whether
acquired by *transfer* under an
established and legallybased procedure, by *deposit*, purchase, *gift* or
bequest. See also ACCESSION.

D Aanwinst

G Erwerbung, Zugang

I Acquisizione

ACCROISSEMENT   9

Ensemble des *documents* entrés
pendant une période donnée dans
un service d'*archives (2)* ou dans un
centre de préarchivage tant par *versement* que par *dépôt, réintégration,*
achat, *don* ou *legs. Voir aussi* (4)
ENREGISTREMENT DES
ACCROISSEMENTS.

R Комплектование архива

S Adquisición, acumulación

ACQUISITION MICROFILMING

The *acquisition* of *microfilm* by
archives (2) to supplement and
complement its own *holdings*.

MICROFILMAGE DE COMPLÉMENT 10

Microfilmage de *documents* conservés
dans un autre service public ou par des
particuliers, effectué par un service
d'*archives (2)* pour compléter ses *fonds*.

(continued)

D [Acquisitiemicroverfilming]

G Ergänzungsverfilmung

I Microfilmatura di complemento

R Комплектование архива микрофильмами

S Microfilme de complemento

ACT

A *document* formally embodying a decision of a legislative body or a public authority; or forming part of a legal transaction and drawn up in due form.

D Akte

G (Notarieller, gerichtlicher) Akt

I Atto, documento

ACTE 11

(1) [*Document* consignant la décision d'un corps législatif ou d'une autorité publique.]
(2) *Document* écrit, établi dans les formes, consignant une décision juridique.

R Акт

S Documento, acta

ACTIVE RECORDS *See* CURRENT RECORDS

ADHESIVE BINDING

A method of *binding* a *volume* without sewing or stitching by applying an adhesive to the spine and cover. Also called perfect binding.

D Lumbeck – bindwijze

G Klebebindung, (Akten)schweissen

I Legatura a colla (o all'americana)

RELIURE PAR COLLAGE 12

Procédé de *reliure* sans couture ni piqûre par application d'un adhésif au dos du *volume*.

R [Бесшовное скрепление документов дела, книги при переплете]

S Encuadernación a la americana

ADMINISTRATIVE MICROFILMING

The use of *microfilm* in the creation and/or use of *current records*.

D [Microverfilming door de administratie]

G Verfilmung für Verwaltungszwecke

I Microfilmatura per uso amministrativo

[Microfilmage administratif] 13

Microfilmage effectué dans les administrations soit comme mode de production de *documents*, soit en remplacement des *originaux*.

R [Микрофильмирование в делопроизводстве]

S Microfilmación administrativo

ADMINISTRATIVE VALUE

The value of *records (1)*/*archives (1)*

[Valeur administrative] 14

Valeur que conserve un *document*

for the conduct of current or future administrative business and/or as evidence thereof. Also called operational value. *See also* FISCAL VALUE: LEGAL VALUE.

D [Administratieve waarde]

G Verwaltungswert, (Verwahrung für) administrative Zwecke

I Validità amministrativa

pour l'administration d'origine ou celle qui lui succède pour le traitement des affaires courantes ou futures. *Voir aussi* (190) VALEUR FISCALE, (260) VALEUR LÉGALE.

R [Практическая ценность документов для учреждения]

S Valor administrativo

ADP *See* AUTOMATIC DATA PROCESSING

ADP RECORDS MANAGEMENT

The specialised area of *records management* concerned with *automatic data processing* (US).

D [Beheer van machine-leesbare dynamische archieven]

G Organisation der Datenverarbeitung

I Gestione di documenti correnti automatizzati

[Gestion des documents informatiques]   **15**
Secteur de la *gestion des documents* spécialisée dans les *archives informatiques.*

R [Организация работы с машиночитаемыми документами]

S Gestión de documentos informáticos, tratamiento de los documentos legibles por máquinas

AERIAL PHOTOGRAPH

Photograph made from a predetermined altitude and in accordance with a plan and scale.

D [Verticale] luchtfoto

G Luftaufnahme

I Fotografia aerea

PHOTOGRAPHIE AÉRIENNE   **16**

Photographie prise d'un engin volant à une altitude déterminée.

R [Фотография, выполненная методом аэрофотосъемки. Аэрофотоснимок]

S Fotografía aérea

AGENCY RECORDS CENTRE

A *records centre* maintained and operated by a non-archival agency, and providing storage for and service only on its own *records (1)* (US).

D Semistatisch archief

G Behördliches Zwischenarchiv; (DDR:) Verwaltungsarchiv

I —

[− − −]   **17**
Centre de préarchivage de *documents* non géré par un service d'*archives (2)* et ne servant qu'à son producteur. (U.S.)

R [Ведомственный архив, архив учреждения]

S Archivo administrativo

AISLE
A principal route through a storage
area providing access to the cross-
aisles or gangways between *rows*
of *shelving.*

D Gang

G (Haupt)gang (im Magazin)

I Corridoio principale

ALLÉE PRINCIPALE DE CIRCULATION
Allée de circulation traversant un   18
magasin d'archives (3) et donnant
accès aux allées de desserte entre
les *épis.*

R Главный проход в архивохранилище

S Pasillo principal

ALIENATION
The loss of *custody* or ownership of
records (1)/archives (1) by their
custodian or owner to someone not
legally entitled to them. *See also*
ESTRAY.

D Vervreemding

G Entfremdung

I —

ALIÉNATION   19
Perte de la garde de *documents* ou
de *fonds d'archives* par l'autorité
responsable soit en vertu d'un acte
législatif spécifique, soit illégale-
ment.

R[(1) Отчуждение, лишение
права собственности на
документы.
(2) Переход документов
к другому выдальцу или
хранителю.]

S Transmisión de fondos

ALPHABETICAL ARRANGEMENT *See* ARRANGEMENT

ANALYTICAL INVENTORY *See* CALENDAR

ANNEXE
(1) *Archives (3)* or *records centre*
usually physically separate from the
principal one and holding overflow
materials or those selected for
storage therein because of their
physical type, frequency of use or
other special characteristics.
(2) Something physically added or
appended to a *document.* Also referred to as an attachment.
See also BRANCH REPOSITORY.

D (1) Hulpdepot
(2) Bijlage

G (1) Aussenstelle
(2) Anlage

I (1) Deposito sussidiario o
succursale
(2) Allegato

(1) DÉPÔT ANNEXE (1)   20
Local de conservation d'*archives (1)*
séparé du *dépôt* principal et destiné
en principe à recueillir certaines
catégories de *documents* de type,
de date, de volume ou d'usage
particulier. *Voir aussi* (50) DÉPÔT
ANNEXE (2).

(2) PIÈCE ANNEXE
Document joint à un autre avec
lequel il possède un rapport de
contenu.

R (1)[Специальное архивохра-
нилище]

(2) Приложение к документу

S (1) Depósito , archivo complementario (anejo)
(2) Documento anejo

20

ANTHROPONYMY *See* ONOMASTICS

APERTURE CARD

A card, usually punched and of a
size and shape suitable for use in
data processing systems, with one
or more rectangular holes specifically designed to hold a *frame* or
frames of *microfilm. See also*
PUNCHED CARD.

D Venster(pons)kaart

G Filmlochkarte, Fensterkarte

I Scheda a fenestra

CARTE À FENÊTRE   21

Carte destinée au traitement automatique normalement munie d'ouver-
tures rectangulaires permettant
l'enchâssement d'une ou de plusieurs
vues de *microfilm. Voir aussi* (382)
CARTE/BANDE PERFORÉE.

R Апертурная карта

S Ficha de ventana

APPRAISAL

A basic archival function of determining the eventual *disposal* of
records based upon their *archival
value*. Also referred to as evaluation, review, selection or selective
retention.

D Selectie

G (Be)Wertung, Wertermittlung

I Selezione

(1) TRI   22

Fonction archivistique fondamentale
déterminant le sort des *documents* à
partir de leur *valeur administrative,
fiscale, légale, probatoire*, d'information et de recherche, présente et
future.

(2) SÉLECTION

Choix, opéré en cours de *tri*, de *documents* d'intérêt particulier, mais
ponctuel, par opposition à l'*échantillonnage* fondé sur la représentative.

R экспертиза ценности
документов

S Seleción

ARCHIVAL HOLDINGS *See* ARCHIVES (1): HOLDINGS

ARCHIVAL INTEGRITY

A basic standard derived from the
principle of provenance and the
registry principle which requires
that an *archive/record group* shall
be preserved in its entirety without division, mutilation, *alienation,*
unauthorised *destruction* or addition,
except by *accrual* or *replevin*, in
order to ensure its full *evidential*
and *informational value.*

[Intégrité des fonds]   23

Norme fondamentale dérivée du
principe de respect des fonds selon
laquelle le *fonds d'archives* doit être
conservé dans son ordre originel et
ne subir ni morcèlement, ni *élimination*
non autorisée, ni addition d'éléments
étrangers, afin de conserver sa valeur
de preuve et d'information.

D [Integriteit van archieven]

G Unverletzlichkeit (eines provenienz-
mässigen Archivbestands)

I Irítegrità degli archivi

R Недробимость архивного
фонда

S Integridad de un fondo

ARCHIVAL JURISDICTION

The jurisdiction, as defined by law
or regulation, exercised by
archives (2) over the creation,
maintenance, use and *disposal* of
the *records (1)* and *archives (1)*
of a predetermined organisation
or institution.

[Compétence des archives]   24

Compétence d'un service d'*archives (2)* définie par la législation ou
la réglementation en ce qui concerne
la création, la *conservation*, les trans-
ferts, les *éliminations* et l'utilisation
des *documents* produits par des
administrations ou des institutions
préalablement désignées.

D [Archiefcompetentie]

G Archivische Zuständigkeit

I Sorveglianza, vigilanza

R Архивное право, компе-
тенциа архивов

S Competencia archivística

ARCHIVAL PRINCIPLES *See* PRINCIPLE OF PROVENANCE:
REGISTRY PRINCIPLE

ARCHIVAL QUALITY

The material properties inherent
in any documentary *medium*
permitting its indefinite *preservation* under controlled
conditions.

[Qualité de conservation]   25

Propriétés matérielles inhérentes
aux *supports* des *documents* permettant leur *conservation* illimitée
dans des conditions d'emmagasinage
contrôlées.

D [Archiefkwaliteit]

G Archivfähigkeit (materielle
Eignung zu dauernder archivi-
scher Verwahrung)

I Stabilità dei supporti dei
   documenti d'archivio

R [Свойство носителей доку-
ментной информации, тре-
бующие специального ре-
жима архивного хранения]

S Cualidad de archivo

ARCHIVAL REPOSITORY *See* ARCHIVES (3)

ARCHIVAL SUCCESSION

The succession of legal jurisdiction over *archives (1)* as the result
of changes in territorial sovereignty.

[– – –]   26

Transfert de la propriété légale
d'*archives (1)* résultant d'un changement de souveraineté territoriale.

(continued)

D Overgang van archieven (op en rechtsopvolger)

G Archivfolge

I –

R –

S Sucesión en la propiedad de un archivo

ARCHIVAL VALUE

Those *values, administrative, fiscal, legal, evidential* and/or *informational*, which justify the indefinite or permanent retention of *records/archives (1)*.

D –

G Archivwert

I Valore archivistico, valore storico/giuridico, valore permanente

VALEUR ARCHIVISTIQUE 27

Valeur de preuve ou d'information qui justifie la *conservation* permanente de *documents* dans une institution d'*archives (2)*.

R [Ценность документов]

S Valor permanente, valor histórico

ARCHIVE

(1) *Archives (1)* originating from a single *provenance* (UK).
See ARCHIVE GROUP: PRINCIPLE OF PROVENANCE (2): RECORD GROUP.
(2) An individual *item* forming a part of *archives (2)* (UK).

D (1) Archief
(2) Archiefstuk

G (1) (Einzelliges) Archiv
(2) Archivdokument, Archivale

I (1) Archivio, fondo, registratura, protocollo (Obsolete)
(2) Unità archivistica, pezzo, documento

[– – –] 28

(1) *Fonds d'archives* de provenance unique (U.K.). *Voir aussi* (30) SÉRIE (1), (367) PRINCIPE DU RESPECT DES FONDS.
(2) Unité d'archives formant une partie des *archives (1)* (U.K.)

R (1) Архивный фонд
(2) Архивные документы

S (1) Fondo
(2) Unidad archivística

ARCHIVE(S) ADMINISTRATION

(1) The theoretical and practical study of policies, procedures and problems relating to archival functions.
(2) The direction and management of *archives (2)*.

ARCHIVISTIQUE 29

(1) Discipline traitant des aspects théoriques et pratiques de la fonction 'archives'.
(2) [Administration et gestion des *archives (2)*.]

(continued)

D (1) Archivistiek
(2) Archiefbeheer

G (1) Archivverwaltungslehre
(2) Archivverwaltung

I (1) Archivistica applicata
(2) Direzione e gestione degli
archivi (2)

R (1) Архивоведение
(2) Управление архивами
Архивное дело

S (1) Archivística, archivología,
archivonomía
(2) Administración de archivos

ARCHIVE(S) AGENCY *See* ARCHIVES (2)

ARCHIVE(S) ARRANGEMENT *See* ARRANGEMENT

ARCHIVE(S) BOX/CONTAINER *See* BOX

ARCHIVE(S) DEPOSITORY *See* ARCHIVES (3)

ARCHIVE GROUP   SÉRIE (1)   30
The primary division in the
arrangement of *archives (1)* at
the level of the independent originating unit or agency. *See also*
RECORD GROUP.

Division primaire à l'intérieur d'un
fonds d'*archives (1)* définie par un
cadre de classement. Voir aussi (389)
SÉRIE (2).

D Archief

G Archivbestand

I Fondo, registratura, archivio

R Архивный фонд

S Sección

ARCHIVE(S) KIT *See* ARCHIVE TEACHING UNIT

ARCHIVE(S) MANAGEMENT *See* ARCHIVE(S) ADMINISTRATION

ARCHIVE(S) MUSEUM   MUSÉE DES ARCHIVES   31
A permanent *exhibition*, composed
mainly of *archives (1)* for educational
and/or cultural purposes.

Exposition permanente organisée
dans un service d'*archives (2)* et
composée principalement de
documents d'archives (1)
choisis à des fins culturelles et
parfois éducatives.

24

(continued)

D Permanente archieftentoon-
   stelling

G Archivausstellung (als
   Dauerausstellung)

I Mostra permanente

R Архивный музей

S Exposición permanente

ARCHIVE(S) TEACHING UNIT

A selction, relating to some historical period, event, movement, or
person, of *facsimiles* of *documents,
copies* of *photographs* and *maps*
for classroom use with explanatory
material for teachers and students.

D Lesmap

G [Dokumentenmappe für Unter-
   richtszwecke]

I Atlante documentario

DOSSIER DE SERVICE ÉDUCATIF   32

Pochette ou *dossier* formé par un
choix de *reproductions* de *documents
d'archives (1)* établi par périodes ou
par thèmes, destiné à des maîtres, à
des étudiants ou à des élèves, et
accompagnées de commentaires.

R Подборка копий докумен-
   тов для учебных целей

S [Selección de documentos,
   realizada con fines didácticos]

ARCHIVES

(1) *Non-current records* preserved,
with or without selection, by those
responsible for their creation or by
their successors in function for their
own use or by an appropriate *archives
(2)* because of their *archival value.*
(2) An institution responsible for the
acquisition, preservation and *communication* of *archives (1):* also called
archival agency (US), archive(s) service, record office. *Archives (1)* and
(2) are also called after the type of
institution whose *archives (1)* they
acquire e.g. college and university
archives, press/radio/television archives. *See also* BUSINESS/CHURCH/
LITERARY ARCHIVES.
(3) A building or part of a building
in which *archives (1)* are preserved
and made available for consultation:
also called archive(s) repository;
archival depository (US).

D (1) Archiefbescheiden,
      archiefstukken
   (2) Archiefdienst

ARCHIVES   33

(1) Ensemble des *documents*, quels
que soient leur date, leur forme et
leur support matériel, produits ou
reçus par toute personne physique
ou morale, et par tout service ou organisme public ou privé, dans l'exercice de leur activité, *documents* soit
conservés par leur créateur ou leurs
successeurs pour leurs besoins propres,
soit transmis à l'institution d'*archives
(2)* compétente en raison de leur
valeur archivistique. Voir aussi (387)
DOCUMENT D'ARCHIVES.
(2) Institution responsable de la prise
en charge, du *traitement*, de l'inventaire,
de la *conservation* et de la *communication* des *archives (1)*, dite aussi service
d'*archives (2).*
(3) Bâtiment ou partie de bâtiment où
sont conservés et communiqués des
archives (1), dit aussi dépôt d'archives.

R (1) Архивные документы,
      Архивный фонд
   (2) Архив, Архивная служба

(continued)

(3) Archiefgebouw,
archiefbewaarplaats

G (1) Archiv, Archivgut
(2) Archiv
(3) Archiv, Archivgebäude

I (1) Archivio
(2) Archivio
(3) Archivio, deposito,
magazzino

(3) Архивохранилище

S (1) Archivo(s) histórico(s)
(2) Archivo
(3) Archivo

ARCHIVIST

A person professionally occupied
in the administration of *archives (1)*
and/or the management of *archives (2)*.
See also RECORDS MANAGER:
MANUSCRIPT CURATOR.

D Archivaris

G Archivar

I Archivista, archivario
(obsolete)

ARCHIVISTE 34

Spécialiste chargé d'une ou de
plusieurs fonctions dans la gestion
d'*archives* (1). *Voir aussi* (393)
RECORDS MANAGER, (281)
CONSERVATEUR DE MANUS-
CRITS.

R Архивист

S Archivero

ARRANGEMENT

(1) The intellectual operations
involved in the organisation of
records (1) / archives (1) based
upon the *principle of provenance*
and the *registry principle,* reflecting
the administrative structure and/or
competence or function of the originating agency. If this is impossible
then an organisation based upon
other criteria adapted to the physical type or form or content of the
documents, such as an alphabetical,
chronological, geographical or subject order, may be used. Arrangement may be carried out at all or
any of the following levels: *repository, record/archive group, sub-group,
class* or *series, item* or *document.*
(2) The physical operations complementary to (1) above such as
numbering, boxing and *shelving.*

CLASSEMENT (1) 35

(1) Opérations intellectuelles effec-
tuées lors du traitement d'un *fonds*
ou d'une partie de *fonds*, basées sur
le *principe du respect des fonds* et
sur le *principe du respect de l'ordre
primitif* reflétant la structure administrative de l'organisme producteur, ou,
en cas d'impossibilité, adaptées au
contenu des *documents* suivant des
critères chronologiques, géographiques,
alphabétiques ou thématiques. Le
classement est applicable à un ou
plusieurs niveaux: *fonds d'archives,*
(fonds secondaires), *séries.*
(2) [Opérations matérielles, complémentaires de (1), comme la *cotation*,
le *conditionnement*, ou le rangement
sur les rayons.]

(continued)

D (1/2) Ordenen

G (1/2) Ordnung, Ordnungsarbeit

I (1) Ordinamento e inventariazione
(2) Condizionamento

R (1) Классификация. Систе-
матизация документов в
пределах архивного фонда
(1/2) Научно-техничиская
обработка архивного фонда

S (1) Clasificación y ordenación
(2) Acondicionamiento

ARRANGEMENT BY ADMINISTRATIVE COMPETENCE *See* ARRANGEMENT

ARRANGEMENT BY ORGANISATIONAL STRUCTURE *See* ARRANGEMENT

ATTACHEMENT *See* ANNEXE (2)

AUDIO-TAPE *See* PHONOTAPE

AUDIO-VISUAL RECORDS/ARCHIVES

Records (1) /archives (1) in
pictorial and/or aural form, re-
gardless of format, including re-
lated *textual records/archives.*
See also FILM ARCHIVES:
ICONOGRAPHIC ARCHIVES:
PHOTOGRAPHIC ARCHIVES:
SOUND ARCHIVES.

D Audiovisuele archiefbescheiden

G Bild-, Film- und Tondokumen-
tation/-archivgut, Audiovisuelle(s)
Dokumentation/Archivgut

I Documenti/archivi audiovisivi

ARCHIVES AUDIO-VISUELLES 36

Ensemble de *documents* consistant
en reproductions d'*images* fixes ou
mobiles et en *enregistrements sonores*
sur tout *support. Voir aussi* (230)
ARCHIVES ICONOGRAPHIQUES,
(353) ARCHIVES PHOTOGRAPHI-
QUES, (499) ENREGISTREMENT
SONORE.

R Аудио-визуальные доку-
менты

S Documentos audiovisuales

AUTHENTICATION

The determination that a *document* or a *reproduction* of a
document is what it purports to
be. Also but incorrectly used as
if synonymous with *certification.*

D [Vaststelling van de authenti-
citeit]

G Echtheitsbestätigung

I Autenticazione

AUTHENTIFICATION 37

Attestation selon laquelle un
document d'archives ou sa
reproduction est authentique.

R Установление достовер-
ности документа

S Autenticación

AUTOCLAVE *See* FUMIGATION CHAMBER

AUTOGRAPH
(1) A *manuscript*, signed or unsigned, in the hand of the author.
(2) A *signature (1)*. *See also* HOLOGRAPH.

D (1) Autograaf
(2) Handtekening

G (1) Autograph
(2) (Eigenhändige) Unterschrift, Autogramm

I (1) Autografo
(2) Firma, sottoscrizione autografa

AUTOGRAPHE   **38**
(1) Texte écrit de la main de son auteur, signé ou non.
(2) *Signature. Voir aussi* (225) OLOGRAPHE.

R (1/2) Автограф

S (1) Autógrafo
(2) Firma autógrafa

AUTOMATIC DATA PROCESSING
Automatic operations, either by mechanical or electronic equipment, permitting the rapid exploitation of large quantities of *data (1)*. Abreviated to ADP.

D Automatische informatiever-werking

G Automatisierte/Elektronische Datenverarbeitung (ADV/EDV)

I Elaborazione automatica di dati

TRAITEMENT AUTOMATIQUE DES DONNÉES   **39**
Opérations automatiques exécutées au moyen d'équipements mécaniques ou électroniques permettant l'exploitation rapide de *données (1)* en grand nombre; souvent abrégé ADP en anglais.

R Автоматическая обработка данных

S Proceso de datos

BACK-TO-BACK ROWS/SHELVING
Two *rows* or *ranges* of *shelving* immediately adjacent to each other along their long axis.

D Rug aan rugstelling

G Doppel(-Regal)reihen

I Fila di scaffalatura bifronte

ÉPI DOUBLE   **40**
Ensemble de *rayonnages* bi-faces (ou à double face) disposés dans l'axe des *tablettes*.

R Сдвоенный стеллаж

S Estantería de doble faz

BARROW PROCESS *See* DEACIDIFICATION

BASE *See* MEDIUM

BAY

A unit of *shelving*, single or double-sided, consisting of horizontal *shelves* between standards, *uprights* or upright frames. Also called compartment (US).
See also BACK-TO-BACK ROWS.

D (Archief)stelling

G Regal(einheit), Stange

I Colonna di scaffaltura, scaffale

TRAVÉE 41

Ensemble de *tablettes* placées entre deux *montants* latéraux et accessibles sur une face (travée simple) ou sur les deux faces (travée double). *Voir aussi* (40) ÉPI DOUBLE.

R Стеллаж

S Estante

BEQUEST

The transfer of *custody* and of title to *documents* by last will and testament.

D Legaat

G Testamentarische Übereignung

I Lascito testamentario, legato

LEGS 42

Don de *documents* résultant d'une disposition testamentaire.

R Передача документов по завещанию

S Legado

BILLS AND VOUCHERS *See* VOUCHER

BINARY NOTATION

A system in *automatic data processing* in which numbers are represented by the two digits 0 and 1. *See also* BIT.

D Binair talstelsel

G Binäre Darstellung, -Schreibweise

I Notazione binaria

NOTATION BINAIRE 43

Dans le *traitement automatique des données,* système selon lequel les nombres sont représentés par les deux chiffres 0 et 1. *Voir aussi* (45) CHIFFRE BINAIRE.

R Двоичная система счисления

S Notación binaria

BINDING

(1) The permanent fastening together usually between covers, of manuscript or printed *sheets* to keep them in a fixed order and to assist in protecting them.
(2) The cover in (1) above.

D (1) Binden
　　(2) Band

RELIURE 44

(1) Fixation, généralement opérée entre deux couvertures de matériaux divers, de *feuilles* manuscrites ou imprimées effectuée en vue de les maintenir ensemble dans un ordre déterminé et d'en assurer la protection.
(2) Couvertures utilisées pour (1).

R (1) Переплетные работы
　　(2) Переплет, обложка

(continued)

G (1) Bindung, Heftung
   (2) Einband

I (1) Legatura
  (2) Copertina, legatura

BIT

In *binary notation,* one of the two
digits 0 and 1. An *abbreviation* of
bi(nary digi)t.

D Bit

G Bit

I Bit

BIT/CHIFFRE BINAIRE   45

En *notation binaire*, l'un des deux
nombres 0 et 1. Forme abrégée de
bi(nary digi)t.

R Бит

S Dígito binario

BOOK BOX *See* BOOK CRADLE

BOOK CRADLE

A device used to hold the *pages* of
a bound *volume* open for *reproduction*
in a level or near-level plane, so that
all parts of the *image* are in focus.

D Boekewip

G Buchwippe

I Compensatore di livello,
  compensatore del piano

PRESSE-LIVRE / APLATISSEUR   46

Appareil utilisé, lors de la *photographie*
pour maintenir en plan horizontal les
pages d'un *volume* ouvert de manière à
placer l'*image* tout entière dans le champ
photographique.

R –

S –

BOOK HOLDER

An adjustable frame or support
placed on a desk or table to hold
a bound *volume*, usually oversize, at an angle convenient for
reading. Also called book rest.

D Lessenaar

G Lesepult

I Leggio

PUPITRE   47

Dispositif placé sur une table permettant de présenter un *volume* selon l'in-
clinaison la plus favorable à la lecture.

R Книгодержатель, подстав-
  ка для чтения книг

S Atril

BOOK REST *See* BOOK HOLDER

BOX

A storage container, variable in terms of composition, construction, and dimensions, intended to protect and facilitate the *shelving (2)* and handling of *records (1)/archives (1)*. See *also* RECORDS CENTRE CARTON/ CONTAINER (US)·

D (Archief)doos

G (Archiv-)Karton, Kasten

I Contenitore, scatola, cassetta, busta, faldone

CARTON 48

Boîte rigide généralement en carton, de forme, de structure et de dimensions variable, destinée à contenir et à protéger des *documents d'archives (1)*, à en faciliter la manutention et le rangement.

R Коробка для хранения документов

S Caja

BOXING

The placing or packing of *records (1) / archives (1)* in boxes in the course of the *arrangement (2)*.

D (In dozen) verpakken

G Kartonieren, in Kartons verpacken

I Condizionamento, imbustamento

MISE EN CARTON 49

Procédé de conditionnement consistant à ranger des *documents d' archives (1)* dans des *cartons* lors de déplacements ou lors du *classement* pour en assurer la protection et une manutention plus aisée.

R Картонирование

S Instalación en cajas

BRANCH REPOSITORY

A sub-division or section of *archives (2)*, physically separate, responsible for the *acquisition, preservation* and *communication* of specified *archives (1)*. See also ANNEXE (1).

D Hulpdepot, dependance

G Zweigarchiv

I Sezione di archivio

DÉPÔT ANNEXE (2) 50

Section ou subdivision d'une institution d'*archives (2)* matériellement séparée et responsable de la *conservation* et de la *communication* d'un ensemble déterminé de *fonds* et de *collections. Voir aussi* (20) DÉPÔT ANNEXE (1).

R Филиал архива

S Depósito complementario, depósito anejo

BREVIATE *See* BRIEF (1)

BRIEF

(1) An open *letter* issued by the papal chancery, sealed with a wax

(1) BREF 51

Lettre (1) issue de la chancellerie pontificale, scellée d'un *sceau (2)*

seal (2) and of less formality than
a *bull (2)*.
(2) A *letter* issued by a lawful
authority to an individual or institution commanding the performance of a specified action. More
usually called a *writ*.
(3) A summary, abstract or abridge-
ment of a *document*.
(4) A summary of the facts of a case
with special reference to the points
of law involved to assist in presenting
the case before a court of law.

secret de cire rouge portant l'empreinte de l'anneau du pêcheur, et moins
solennelle qu'une *bulle (2)*.
(2) MANDEMENT
Lettre (1) émise par une autorité re-
quérant l'exécution d'un ordre et
adressée soit à une institution, soit
à un groupe spécifique de personnes.
(3) [Résumé, sommaire d'un
document].
(4) [Exposé sommaire des faits d'un
procès avec référence spéciale à la
législation, destiné à faciliter la présentation d'une cause devant une
instance judiciaire, U.K.]

D (1) Breve
   (2) Bevelschrift
   (3) Resumé, uittreksel, regest
   (4) –

G (1) Breve
   (2) Verfügung
   (3) Inhaltsangabe, Regest
   (4) Prozess-Instruktion

I (1) Breve
   (2) Lettera ufficiale, mandato
   (3) Regesto, Sunto
   (4) Sommario

R (1) Бреве
   (2) Повестка
   (3) экстракт документа

S (1) Breve
   (2) Mandato, orden
   (3) Resumen
   (4) Sumario

BULL

(1) A round metal *seal (2)* attached
to a *document* of great formality,
especially the leaden *seal (2)*
attached to a certain type of papal
charter.
(2) A *document* so sealed.

D (1/2) Bul

G (1/2) Bulle

I (1) Bolla
   (2) Bolla, privilegio solenne,
      lettera grazioso, diploma,
      lettera esecutoria o
      mandato

BULLE 52

(1) *Sceau (2)* métallique de forme
ronde attaché à un *document* solennel
et particulièrement le *sceau* de plomb
appendu à certains *actes* pontificaux.
(2) *Acte* ainsi scellé.

R (1/2) Булла

S (1) Bula (Papal), sello metálico
   (2) Documento con bula (Papal)
      o sello metálico

BUNDLE

A storage unit consisting of a number of individual *documents,* whether or not related by content or function, normally tied together by string, tape, or the like. A bundle may be 'original' i.e. in that form and order of *documents* as received in *archives (3)* or may be so formed in the course of *arrangement.*

D Bundel

G Bündel, Büschel

I Busta (Roma), filza (Firenze). mazzo (Torino), fascio (Napoli)

LIASSE   53

Unité matérielle de *conservation* d'*archives (1)* formée par un ensemble de *documents* sanglés ou ficelés; elle est 'originale', si elle provient dans sa forme de l'organisme producteur, ou elle peut être formée en cours de *classement.*

R Связка документов, дело

S Legajo, mazo

BUSINESS ARCHIVES

(1) *Archives (1)* of business and commercial organisations.
(2) *Archives (2)* responsible for the *acquisition, preservation* and *communication* of such *archives (1).*

D (1) Bedrijfsarchief
(2) Bedrijfsarchief(dienst)

G (1) Wirtschaftsarchiv(gut)
(2) Wirtschaftsarchiv(e)

I (1) Archivi delle imprese
(2) Archivi economici

ARCHIVES ÉCONOMIQUES   54

(1) *Archives (1)* issues des activités des entreprises et des établissements industriels, commerciaux et bancaires.
(2) Institution d'*archives (2)* établie pour assurer la collecte, la *conservation* et la *communication* de ces *archives (1).*

R (1) Архивные фонды предприятий
(2) Архивы предприятий, экономические архивы

S (1/2) Archivos de empresa

BYTE

(1) A sequence of adjacent *bits,* usually eight, operated upon as a unit in *automatic data processing* and often shorter than a *computer word.*
(2) The representation of a *character* in *automatic data processing.*

D Byte

G (1/2) Byte

I (1/2) Byte

OCTET   55

(1) Chaîne d'éléments binaires, généralement au nombre de huit, traité comme une unité dans le *traitement automatique des données* et qui est souvent plus courte qu'un *mot.*
(2) Représentation d'un *caractère* en *traitement automatique des données.*

R Байт

S (1/2) Octeto

CALENDAR

(1) A list, usually in chronological order, of précis of individual *documents* in the same *series* or of a specified kind from a variety of sources, giving all content and material *information* essential to the user.
(2) A list, chronologically or alphabetically arranged, with essential personal details of persons committed for trial in a court of law or held in a prison.

D (1) Regenstenlijst
  (2) [Register van veroordeelden]

G (1/2) Regesten(-Repertorium, -Werk)

I (1) Registri cronologici, spogli (Firenze)
  (2) Ruolo generale o di udienza (tribunale), rubrica degli imputati (pretura), matricola (carceraria)

CAMERA-PROCESSOR

A device which combines the function of creating a photographic *image* on *film* and of *processing (2)* the exposed *film*.

D Instant camera

G Processor-Kamera

I Apparechia da ripresa e sviluppo

CARBON COPY

A *copy* of a *document* created simultaneously with the *original manuscript* or *typescript* by the use of an intermediate sheet of carbon paper or of self-carboned paper.

D Doorslag

G Durchschlag, Kohlekopie

I Copia con carta carbone

(1) REGESTE   56

Liste généralement chronologique d'*analyses* de *documents* appartenant à un même *fonds* ou portant sur un sujet donné et fournissant sur leur contenu et leur forme toutes les *informations* nécessaires à la recherche.
(2) [Registre de citations]
Liste chronologique ou alphabétique comportant les données essentielles sur les personnes citées en jugement devant un tribunal.(U.K.)
(3) REGISTRE D'ÉCROU
Liste chronologique ou alphabétique des personnes détenues en prison (F.)

R (1/2) Perест

S (1) Regesta
  (2) –

CAMÉRA À DÉVELOPPEMENT INTÉGRÉ

Caméra à laquelle est adjoint un   57
système de développement automatique du *film*, lui permettant de produire un *négatif* immédiat.

R –

S Cámara procesadora

CARBONE, PELURE, DOUBLE   58

Copie établie en même temps que l'*original* manuscrit ou dactylographié, obtenue grâce à une *feuille* de papier *carbone* intercalaire.

R Копия документа, выполненная с помощью копировальной бумаги

S Copia al carbón

CARD INDEX

An *index* recorded on cards of uniform size, arranged in a predetermined order, e.g. alphabetical, numerical, subject.

D Kaartsysteem

G Kartei

I Schedario

CARTOGRAPHIC RECORDS/ ARCHIVES

Records (1)/archives (1) containing *information* depicting in graphic or photogrammetric form, a portion of the linear surface of the earth or of a heavenly body, such as *maps, charts, plans* and related materials (globes, topographic and hydrographic *charts*, cartograms, relief models, and *aerial photographs*), including related *textual records/archives*.

D Cartografische archiefbescheiden

G Kartographisches Archivgut, Plankammer

I Archivio cartografico

CARTRIDGE

A closed container of *film* or of *magnetic tape*, designed for loading and unloading in a *reader*, projector, recorder or computer tape drive, without prior threading or rewinding. A double-cored cartridge is called a cassette.

D Cartridge

G Kassette

I Cassetta, caricotore

CARTULARY

A *register*, usually in *volume* form, of copies of *charters, title*

FICHIER 59

Ensemble de fiches de format uniforme classées dans un ordre préétabli, alphabétique, numérique, méthodique.

R Карточный указатель Картотека

S Fichero

ARCHIVES CARTOGRAPHIQUES 60

Fonds ou *collections* de *documents* contenant des informations qui, sous une forme graphique ou photogrammétrique, représentent une portion de surface terrestre ou de corps céleste, telles que *cartes, plans* et objets apparentés (globes, plans topographiques et hydrographiques, cartogrammes, maquettes en relief, *photographies aériennes, dessins techniques*). Dits aussi *documents* cartographiques, ou *cartes* et *plans*.

R Картографические документы

S Documentos/archivos cartográficos

CHARGEUR 61

Appareil de conditionnement clos à un seul noyau contenant un *microfilm* ou une *bande magnétique*, conçu pour charger ou décharger *l'appareil de lecture*, de projection, d'enregistrement ou l'*ordinateur*. Le chargeur à deux noyaux est appelé *cassette*.

R Кассета

S Cartucho

CARTULAIRE 62

Recueil manuscrit, généralement en forme de *volume*, parfois de *rouleau*,

(continued)

deeds, grants of privileges and
other documents of significance
belonging to a person, family or
institution.

D Cartularium

G Kopiar, Kopialbuch

I Cartolario, cartulario,
cartario

contenant la transcription de titres ou
de documents jugés importants, le
plus souvent des chartes (d'où son
nom), reçus par une personne
physique ou morale.

R Картулярий

S Cartulario

CASE PAPERS/FILES

Files (1) or (2) relating to a
specific action, event, person,
place, project, or other subject.
Sometimes referred to as a project file or dossier. In UK usage,
particular instance papers: in
Canadian usage, transactional
files.

D Dossier

G Sachakten, Einzelfallakten

I Fascicolo, pratica, incarta-
mento, carpetta

DOSSIER DE DOCUMENTATION 63

Ensemble de documents, de provenances diverses, réunis artificielle-
ment à des fins de documentation
et groupés par sujet, tels que actions,
événements, lieux, personnes, projets.

R Дело

S Expediente

CASH BOOK

A volume in which are entered
in chronological order all receipts
and disbursements of money.

D Kasboek

G Kassentagebuch, -journal

I Libro di cassa, libro giornale

LIVRE DE CAISSE 64

Registre de comptabilité où sont
inscrits dans l'ordre chronologique
toutes les entrées et sorties d'argent
d'une personne ou d'un organisme.

R Кассовая книга

S Libro de caja

CASING

The addition of a separately made
cover to the body of a volume.

D [Van een band voorzien]

G Einhängen

I Incartonatura

CARTONNAGE 65

Procédé de reliure utilisant une
couverture préfabriquée fixée à
la colle ou par des pinces.

R Переплетные работы

S Poner tapas

CASSETTE *See* CARTRIDGE

CATALOGUE

An archival *finding aid* describing
individual *documents* of a specific
type e.g *maps, documents* brought
together for a specific purpose e.g.
an *exhibition* or relating to a
defined subject.

D Catalogus

G Katalog

I Catalogo

CATALOGUE 66

Instrument de recherche fournissant
le description *pièce* à *pièce* d'un type
spécifique de *documents*, comme les
cartes et *plans*, ou de *documents*
réunis dans un dessein particulier
(*expositions*) ou se rapportant à un
thème déterminé.

R Архивный каталог

S Catálogo

CATALOGUE ROOM *See* INVENTORY ROOM

CENSUS RETURN/SCHEDULE

An official, usually periodic,
list of persons and/or property
with varying degrees of descriptive detail.

D [Bevolkingsregister]

G Volkszählungsliste

I Censimento

LISTE DE RECENSEMENT / 67
DE DÉNOMBREMENT

Relevé administratif, généralement
périodique, de personnes, assorti de
détails de précision variable.

R Перепись населения

S Censo, catastro

CENTRE CARTON *See* RECORDS CENTRE CARTON/CONTAINER

CENTRAL ARCHIVES

Archives (2) responsible for
archives (1) of a national/
federal or state government.
Also designated as general state
archives or *national archives.*
See also REGIONAL ARCHIVES.

D [Centraal archief]

G Zentralarchiv(e)

I Archivio centrale dello stato,
archivio nazionale

ARCHIVES CENTRALES / NATIONALES

Institution d'*archives (2)* responsa- 68
ble des *archives (1)* d'un gouvernement
national ou fédéral. Dites *archives
nationales* (F) ou *archives générales*
(B).

R Центральный архив

S Archivo nacional, archivo general

CENTRAL FILES

The *records (1)* or *files (1)* of one
or several offices or organisational
units physically and/or functionally

[Archives de service regroupées] 69

Documents et *dossiers* produits par
les divers bureaux et services d'une
administration regroupés pour des

(continued)

centralised and supervised in one location.

D [Centraal gevormde dossiers]

G Zentralakten, -Register

I Archivo generale di un amministrazione, registratura centrale

commodités de *conservation* et d'utilisation.

R Архив, Архив ведомства

S Archivo central

CENTRAL PROCESSING UNIT

That part of a *computer* in which *processing (3)* takes place including the control and arithmetic units and internal *memory* as distinct from a *peripheral.* Abbreviated as CPU. Also called mainframe. *See also* MICRO-PROCESSOR.

D Centrale verwerkingseenheid

G Zentraleinheit

I Unità centrale di elaborazione

UNITÉ CENTRALE   70

Partie de l'*ordinateur* où s'effectuent les traitements, comprenant les organes centraux de contrôle et de calcul, lesquels prennent en charge et exécutent les instructions, et la *mémoire (2)* interne: s'oppose au *périphérique. Voir aussi* (305) MICROPROCESSEUR.

R Центральный процессор

S Unidad central de proceso

CENTRAL REGISTRY *See* REGISTRY

CERTIFICATION

(1) The act of attesting the official character of a *document* or of a *copy* thereof.
(2) The *document* containing such an attestation.
See also AUTHENTICATION.

D (1) Certificatie
   (2) Authentiek afschrift

G (1) Beglaubigung
   (2) Beglaubigung, Beglaubigte Abschrift

I (1) Certificazione
   (2) Certificato

AUTHENTICATION   71

(1) Attestation du caractère officiel d'un *document original* ou de sa *copie.*
(2) *Document* contenant cette attestation.

R (1) Удостоверение документа

   (2) Удостоверенный документ

S (1) Autenticación, certificación legalización
   (2) Certificado

CERTIFIED COPY *See* CERTIFICATION (2)

CERTIFIED EXTRACT *See* EXTRACT (2)

CHARACTER
A letter, digit or other symbol used in the representation of *data (1)*.

D Teken, karakter

G Zeichen

I Carattere

CHARACTÈRE   72
Lettre, chiffre ou autre symbole employé conventionnellement pour représenter une *donnée (1)*.

R Знак, символ

S Carácter

CHARGE-OUT
(1) The act of recording the removal from storage of *documents* within *archives (3)*. In UK, production.
(2) The *document* used to record this action. *See also* PRODUCTION TICKET.

D (1) Lichten, uitlichten
   (2) [Aanvraagbriefje, vlag]

G (1) Aushebung (von Archivalien), (interne) Ausleihe
   (2) Leihzettel, Bestellzettel

I (1) Registrazione del prelievo di documenti dal deposito archivistico
   (2) Schedi di richiamo

[– – –]   73
(1) Action de consigner le déplacement d'un *document* à l'intérieur d'une institution.
(2) FICHE DE DÉPLACEMENT, FANTÔME.
Document utilisé pour consigner un déplacement, destiné à permettre le contrôle des mouvements effectués.

R (1) Выдача документов из архивохранилища
   (2) Книга учета выдачи документов из архивохранилища

S Papeleta de pedido

CHART
A *map* designed primarily for navigation, either nautical or aeronautical.

D Kaart

G Navigationskarte

I Carta di navigazione

CARTE DE NAVIGATION   74
Carte conçue essentiellement pour la navigation maritime, fluviale ou aérienne.

R Навигационная карта

S Carta de navegación

CHARTER
A *document*, usually sealed, granting specific rights, setting forth aims and principles, embodying formal agreements, authorising

CHARTE   75
Document consignant un *acte* juridique manifestant la volonté de son auteur, généralement scellé.

(continued)

special privileges or exemptions
or, in English law, a *deed*, con-
veyance, or similar *document*.

D CHarter

G Urkunde

I Documento, charta, diploma

R Жалованная грамота
Хартия

S Diploma

CHECKLIST
A *list,* usually for an individual
accession, prepared by the trans-
ferring agency or *archives (2)*
for purposes of identification
and control.

D Plaatsingslijst

G (Ablieferungs-, Kontroll-)
Liste

I Elenco di versamento

[− − −] 76

(1) *Instrument de recherche* établi
par le service d'*archives (2)* récepteur
sous forme d'une liste préliminaire de
documents, assortie ou non d'une
analyse sommaire de leur contenu.
(2) [Liste de contrôle]
Liste de *documents* ou d'*articles*
établie à des fins d'identification et
de contrôle.

R [(1) Предварительная опись
документов, поступающих
на хранение]
(2) Краткая опись доку-
ментов

S Inventario somero

CHIROGRAPH
A legally binding agreement between two or more parties in two
or more *originals* or *copies,* each
having their edges serrated,
indented or otherwise marked
for *authentication.* The term by
itself is used without specific reference to the form and content
of the *document* and, in more
recent times, without serration,
indenting or other marking. Also
called indenture.

D Chirograaf

G Chirograph, Kerbzettel

I Carta partita

CHARTE-PARTIE 77
Document sur lequel le texte d'un
contrat est transcrit autant de fois
qu'il y a de parties contractantes,
chaque texte, séparé de l'autre par
un dessin ou une devise, étant censé,
après découpage plus ou moins
irrégulier de ses bords, présenter
toute garantie d'*authenticité* grâce
à la juxtaposition exacte des parties découpées; dit aussi chiro-
graphe.

R —

S Carta partida

CHRON FILE *See* CHRONOLOGICAL FILE

CHRONO *See* CHRONOLOGICAL FILE

CHRONOLOGICAL ARRANGEMENT *See* ARRANGEMENT

CHRONOLOGICAL FILE

A *file (1)* containing *copies* of *documents* arranged in chronological order. Also referred to as chron file, chrono, day file, or reading file, and, in Canadian usage, as a continuity file.

D Chronologisch geordend dossier

G Auslaufserie, Durchschlagserie

I –

CHRONO, PELURIER   78

Dossier (1) contenant une série chronologique de *copies* de *documents* (*correspondance* au départ, parfois à l'arrivée).

R [Дело копий документов, расположенных в хронологическом порядке]

S Serie cronológica

CHRONOLOGICAL INVENTORY/LIST

An *inventory (1)/list* in which the *entries* are made in a chronological order, which may not be in the original order.

D Chronologische inventaris

G Chronologische Liste

I Elenco cronologico, repertorio chronologico

RÉPERTOIRE CHRONOLOGIQUE   79

Répertoire énumérant les *articles* dans un ordre chronologique, parfois indépendant de l'ordre primitif.

R [Архивная опись, построенная по хронологии]

S Inventario cronológico

CHRONOLOGY

(1) The science of measuring time in fixed periods and of identifying and comparing dates expressed in various styles or calendars.
(2) The selection and arrangement of dates and events.

D (1) Chronologie, tijdrekenkunde
   (2) Chronologie

G (1) Chronologie, Zeitrechnungslehre
   (2) Chronologie, zeitliche Abfolge

I (1) Cronologia
   (2) Tavola cronologica

CHRONOLOGIE   80

(1) Science de la mesure et de la division du temps appliquée à l'identification et à la comparaison des dates exprimées dans des calendriers différents.
(2) Ensemble de dates et d'événements sélectionnés, classés dans l'ordre chronologique.

R (1) Хронология
   (2) Хроника событий

S (1) Cronología
   (2) Tabla cronológica

CHURCH ARCHIVES

(1) *Archives (1)* of religious
institutions and organisations.
(2) *Archives (2)* responsible for
the *acquisition, preservation*, and
communication of such *archives
(1)*. Also referred to as ecclesiastical
archives.

D (1) Kerkarchief
  (2) Kerkelijke archiefdienst

G (1) Kirchliches Archivgut
  (2) Kirchenarchiv(e)

I (1/2) Archivio ecclesiastico

ARCHIVES CULTUELLES

(1) *Archives (1)* d'institutions
religieuses chrétiennes.
(2) Institution d'*archives (2)*
chargée de la collecte, de la
conservation et de la *communication* de ce type d'*archives (1)*.

R (1) Документы религиоз-
  ных учреждений
  (2) Церковные архивы

S (1/2) Archivos eclesiásticos

CIM *See* COMPUTER INPUT MICROFILM/MICROFORM

CINE/CINEMATOGRAPH FILM *See* MOTIONS PICTURE(S)

CIPHER

(1) A system of writing based on
a key, or set of predetermined
rules or symbols, used for secret
communication.
(2) A message in such writing.
(3) The key to such a system of
writing. Also referred to as *code*.

D (1/2) Geheimschrift, cijfer
  (3) (Cijfer)code

G (1) Chiffre, Code
  (2) Chiffrierter Text
  (3) Chiffrierschlüssel, Code

I (1) Cifra, scrittura in cifra
    o cifrata
  (2) Messagio cifrato, lettera
    in cifra
  (3) Cifrario, codice di chifratura
    e decifrazione, chiave critto-
    grafica

CHIFFRE

(1) Système d'écriture établi à
partir d'une clé ou sur des règles ou
symboles préalablement choisis,
destiné à des communications
secrètes.
(2) [Message ainsi chiffré U.K., U.S.]
(3) Code, clé, permettant de déchiffrer
ce système d'écriture.

R (1) Код, шифр
  (2) Закодированный текст,
  шифровка
  (3) Код, Ключ к шифру

S (1) Cifra, escritura cifrada
  (2) Cifra, texto cifrado
  (3) Cifra, clave, código

CIVIL REGISTER(S)

Register(s) established and kept
by a competent authority recording

REGISTRES D'ÉTAT CIVIL

Registres établis et conservés par
une autorité publique pour consigner

(continued)

chronologically births, marriages and deaths and possibly other data. In US called vital statistics.
See also PARISH REGISTER(S).

chronologiquement les naissances, les mariages et les décès, et parfois d'autres données (légitimations, reconnaissance de paternité, divorces). *Voir* (342) REGISTRE PAROISSIAL.

D Register(s) van de burgerlijke stand

G Zivilstandsregister, Standesregister

I Registro(i) di stato civile

R (1) Книги записи актов гражданского состояния
(2) Метрическая книга

S Registro civil

CLAM SHELL CASE *See* DOCUMENT CASE

CLASS

An identifiable and self-contained sub-division of an *archive group* consisting of a number of *items* with one or more common characteristics (UK). Generally equivalent to *series*.

D Serie

G Gruppe, Abteilung

I Serie, classe

[− − −] 84

Ensemble d'*articles* appartenant à un *fonds* regroupés en fonction d'une ou de plusieurs caractéristiques communes; généralement équivalent à la *série* (U.K.)

R Класс, группа

S Sub-serie

CLASS LIST

A *list* of the *items* in a *class* in numerical order with sufficient detail to distinguish one *item* from another (UK). *See also* INVENTORY (1).

D [Plaatsingslijst van een serie]

G [Aktenliste]

I Inventario di una serie

RÉPERTOIRE NUMÉRIQUE 85

Liste d'*articles* présentée dans l'ordre numérique des *cotes* et comportant les indications nécessaires à l'identification de chacun d'eux. *Voir* (248) INVENTAIRE (1).

R [Номерная опись документов]

S Inventario somero

CLASSIFICATION

(1) The preparation of a *filing plan/system* or *classification scheme* for *records (1)/archives (1)* and the placing of *series* and/ or *items* within such a plan/system

[Planification des classements] 86

Préparation d'un *cadre de classement* d'*archives (2)* en vue de la répartition des *articles* conformément à ce cadre. *Voir aussi* (35) CLASSEMENT (1).

(continued)

or scheme. *See also* ARRANGEMENT.
(2) *See* SECURITY CLASSIFI-
CATION.

D Classificatie

G Klassifikation, Klassifizieren

I Classificazione

R Классификация документов

S Clasificación

CLASSIFICATION PLAN *See* FILING PLAN/SYSTEM

CLASSIFICATION SCHEME
A pattern of arrangement of
archives (1), by *groups, series*
and *items* (not US).

D Ordeningsplan, archiefschema

G Klassifikationsschema, -plan

I Schema di classificazione

CADRE DE CLASSEMENT   87
Plan directeur établi pour le *classement* de l'ensemble des *documents*
conservés dans un service d'*archives
(2)* par *fonds, séries* et *sous-séries*.

R Схема классификации
документов

S Cuadro de clasificación

CLASSIFIED INFORMATION/RECORDS *See* SECURITY CLASSIFICATION

CLEANING
The removal of foreign matter
from *documents* to assist in
their *preservation*.

D Schoonmaken

G Reinigung

I Pulitura

NETTOYAGE   88
Elimination de matières étrangères
sur les *documents* pour contribuer
à leur *conservation*.

R Очистка, обеспыливание
документов

S Limpieza de los documentos,
abstersión

CLEARANCE
An administrative determination
that an individual may have *access*
to restricted *records (1)* or *information* of a specified category.
See also RESTRICTED ACCESS.

D Toestemming voor raadpleging

G Ausnahmegenehmigung

I —

[Accès par dérogation]   89
Autorisation administrative exception-
nelle de *communication* d'un document par dérogation aux lois ou
règlements qui interdisent normalement cette *communication. Voir
aussi* (418) RESTRICTION DE
COMMUNICABILITÉ.

R [Допуск к документам ограниченного пользования]

S Autorización de consulta

44

CLOSED FILE

(1) A *file (1)* or *(2)* relating to a
matter on which action has been
completed and to which further
documents are not likely to be
added.
(2) A *file (1)* or *(2)* with restrictions as to *access* as distinct from
open file (2).

D (1) Afgesloten dossier
(2) Gesloten dossier

G (1) Geschlossene Akte(n)
(2) Verschlußsachen, -akte(n)

I (2) Documenti non consultabili,
documenti riservati e/o
segreti, protocollo riservato

DOSSIER CLOS 90

(1) *Dossier (1)* ou *(2)* relatif à une
affaire réglée et non susceptible
d'*accroissement*.
(2) [*Dossier (1)* ou *(2)* frappé
d'une restriction de *communication*.]

R (1) [Дело, законченное
производством]
(2) Дело, ограниченного
допуска

S (1) Expediente concluso
(2) Fichero con etiqueta de cola

CLOSED RECORD GROUP

A *record group* to which further
records (1) are not likely to be
added because of the abolition of
the agency, major administrative
reorganisation or basic change in
the *filing plan/system*.

D [Afgesloten archiefbestand]

G Geschlossener Bestand

I Fondo chiuso

SÉRIE CLOSE 91

Série ayant cessé de s'accroître en
raison soit de la suppression ou d'une
réorganisation interne profonde de
l'administration productrice des
documents qui la composent, soit
d'un changement du système de
classement.

R Закрытый архивный фонд,
некомплектующийся архив-
ный фонд

S Fondo cerrado

CODE

(1) In *automatic data processing*
a set of rules for representing
data (1), *characters* or instructions.
(2) *See* CIPHER (3).

D Code

G Code, Schlüssel

I Codice

CODE 92

(1) En *traitement automatique des
données*, ensemble conventionnel de
règles de représentation des *données
(1)*, des *caractères* ou d'instructions.
(2) *Voir* (82) CHIFFRE (3).

R Код

S Código

COLLECTION

(1) An artificial *accumulation* of
documents of any *provenance*
brought together on the basis of

COLLECTION 93

(1) Réunion artificielle de *documents*
de toute *provenance*, groupés en
fonction d'une caractéristique com-

some common characteristic, e.g.
way of acquisition, subject,
language, *medium*, type of *document*, name of collector.
(2) A body of *documents* comprising
a *record/archive group* with other
related materials of different
provenance(s).
(3) A loose usage for *private
records/archives*.
See also FAMILY (AND ESTATE)
ARCHIVES: MANUSCRIPT
COLLECTIONS: PAPERS.

D (1) Verzameling
  (2) –
  (3) Collectie

G (1) Sammlung, Sammelbestand
  (2) Mischbestand
  (3) Nachlaß

I (1) Collezione
  (2) Miscellanea, raccolta,
      collezione

mune, telle que mode d'acquisition,
thème, langue, *support*, type de
document, collectionneur. Ce terme
s'oppose à *fonds*.
(2) [Ensemble de *documents* juxtaposant un *fonds d'archives* et des *documents* complémentaires de diverses
provenances.]
(3) [Terme désignant parfois les
archives privées.]
Voir aussi (175) ARCHIVES DE
FAMILLES, (279) MANUSCRIT,
(338) PAPIERS, (389) SÉRIE (2).

R (1/2) Архивная коллекция,
    Рукописное собрание,
    (3) Персональное собрание

S (1/2/3) Colección

COLLECTIVE RECORD GROUP
A type of *record group* which, for
convenience, brings together the
records (1) of a number of relatively small and/or short-lived agencies
that have an administrative or
functional relationship, the
records (1) of each such agency
constituting a separate *sub-group*
(US). *See also* GENERAL RECORD
GROUP: RECORD GROUP.

D Fonds

G Zusammengefaßter Bestand,
  Sammelbestand, Beständegruppe

I –

[Groupement de fonds] 94
Ensemble de petits *fonds* regroupant
pour des raisons de convenance les
documents créés par plusieurs administrations ou services connexes,
éphémères et de compétence peu
étendue; les *fonds* créés par chacune
de ces administrations constituent
à l'intérieur de ce groupement une
série (2) distincte (US). *Voir aussi*
(212) ARCHIVES DE CABINET,
(389) SÉRIE (2).

R Объединенный архивный
   фонд
S –

COM *See* COMPUTER OUTPUT MICROFILM/MICROFORM

COMMON RECORDS SCHEDULE *See* GENERAL RECORDS SCHEDULE

COMMONPLACE BOOK

A *volume* in which is entered, with or without arrangement, *information* of any kind to be remembered or referred to by the compiler. Also called memorandum book.

D Memoriaal

G Mischbuch

I Quaderno di apunti

AIDE-MÉMOIRE   95

Carnet ou *volume* dans lequel un compilateur inscrit, avec ou sans ordre, des informations de toute nature lui servant de mémoire ou de référence.

R —

S Memorandum, libro de notas de familia

COMMUNICATION

A basic archival function of making available and promoting the wider use of *records (1)/ archives (1)* by the preparation and publication of *finding aids,* the provision of *reference service*, the organisation of *exhibitions, documentary publications,* lectures and other cultural and educational activities.

D [Toegankelijk maken en beschikbaar stellen]

G Erschließung

I Comunicazione

[– – –]   96

Fonction archivistique fondamentale destinée à rendre accessible et à promouvoir une utilisation plus large des *documents d'archives (1)* par la préparation et la publication d'*instruments de recherche,* par l'organisation d'un *service de renseignements,* d'un *service éducatif,* d'*expositions,* par la *publication de textes,* par des conférences et d'autres activités éducatives et culturelles.

R Научно-информационная деятельность архива

S Información

COMPACT SHELVING

A system of mobile *shelving (1)* intended to save space and/or guarantee security comprising moveable *back-to-back rows*, actuated manually or electrically, either horizontally on rails or rotating through a quarter-circle on a pivot.

D Compactusberging

G Compactus-, Kompakt-Regal(system)

I Compactus (on rails), Compact (on pivot)

RAYONNAGE DENSE   97

Système de *rayonnage* mobile conçu pour accroître la place disponible ou la sécurité et composé d'*épis* déplaçables à la main ou électriquement soit horizontalement sur des rails, soit en quart de cercle sur des gonds. Compactus (B).

R Стеллажное оборудование типа "компактус"

S 'Compactus', estantería densa

COMPARTMENT *See* BAY

COMPUTER

A machine for processing *data (1)* under the control of recorded instructions without intervention of a human operator during operation. *See also* MICRO-COMPUTER: MINICOMPUTER.

D Computer, elektronische rekenmachine

G Computer, Rechner

I Elaboratore

ORDINATEUR 98

Machine de *traitement automatique des données* commandée par des instructions enregistrées en *mémoire (2)* interne. *Voir* (305) MICRO-ORDINATEUR, (306) MINIORDINATEUR.

R Вычислительная машина

S Ordenador

COMPUTER INPUT MICROFILM/ MICROFORM

Microfilm/microform used to input or re-input *data (1)* to a *computer.* Abbreviated as CIM. *See also* COMPUTER OUTPUT MICROFILM/MICROFORM.

D Computer input microfilm/ microform

G CIM (Dateneingabe über Mikrofilm/Mikroformen)

I Entrata dell' elaboratore su microfilm/microscheda

CIM 99

Microfilm ou *microforme* utilisé pour introduire des *données (1)* dans un *ordinateur. Voir* (100) COM.

R —

S Entrada de ordenador en microfilme/microforma

COMPUTER OUTPUT MICROFILM/ MICROFORM

Computer output produced directly on to *microfilm/microform*, without *paper printout* as an intermediary. The term may also be used to designate the equipment producing the *microform* or the process as a whole. Abbreviated as COM.

D Computer output microfilm/ microform

G COM (Datenausgabe über Mikrofilm/Mikroformen)

I COM

COMPOSITION PAR ORDINATEUR 100 SUR MICROFORME/COM

Produit de sortie d'un *ordinateur* sur *microforme* sans imprimé intermédiaire. Abréviation de 'computer output microfilm'.

R —

S Salida de ordenador en microfilme o microforma (SOM)

COMPUTER PROGRAM

A sequence of instructions or statements in a form acceptable to a *computer* prepared in order to achieve a particular result.

D Computerprogramma

G (Computer-)Programm

I Programma dell'elaboratore

PROGRAMME D'ORDINATEUR 101

Ensemble ordonné d'instructions et d'expressions mises sous forme acceptable par un *ordinateur* et correspondant à la formulation d'un traitement.

R Программа для вычислительной машины

S Programa

COMPUTER WORD

A sequence of *bits* or *characters* treated as a unit and capable of being stored in one *computer* location.

D Computerwoord

G (Computer-)Wort

I Parola per l'elaboratore

MOT 102

Chaîne d'éléments binaires ou de *caractères* constituant dans un *ordinateur* une unité soit technologique, soit sémantique.

R машинное слово

S —

CONCORDANCE

A *finding aid*, in two columns, establishing the relationship between the past and present *reference numbers* of individual *items*.

D Concordantie

G Konkordanz

I Tavola di concordanza, tavola di raffronto

TABLE DE CONCORDANCE 103

Instrument de recherche établi dans le cas où un *fonds* ou une partie de fonds a reçu successivement deux ou plusieurs *cotations* différentes, et présentant face à face sur deux ou plusieurs colonnes la correspondance entre *cotes* anciennes et *cotes* nouvelles.

R Переводная таблица архивных шифров

S Tabla de concordancias

CONFIDENTIALITY

The quality or property of *privacy* or secrecy attaching to certain *information* and/or *records (1)* thereby limiting *access*.

D Vertrouwelijkheid

G Vertraulichkeit

I Riservatezza

SECRET 104

Caractère confidentiel attaché à certains *documents* dépendant de l'information qu'ils continnent et limitant leur *communicabilité*.

R [Документы, информация ограниченного пользования]

S Reserva

CONFLICTING ARCHIVAL CLAIMS

Conflicting claims of political or administrative entities regarding legal title to, *custody* of, and/or *access* to *archives (1)* especially following changes in sovereignty, including decolonization and changes in territorial organisation. *See also* REMOVED ARCHIVES.

D [Omstreden aanspraken op archieven]

G Archivische Zuständigkeits- und Eigentums-Konflikte

I Contenzioso archivistico

CONTENTIEUX ARCHIVISTIQUE 105

Litige entre entités politiques ou administratives au sujet du droit de propriété, de garde et d'*accès* à des *archives (1)*, notamment à la suite de changements de souveraineté, y compris la décolonisation, ou à la suite de réorganisations territoriales. Englobe parfois les litiges entre *lecteurs* ou propriétaires d'*archives privées* et l'administration des *archives (2)*.

R [Правовые споры о принадлежности, месте хранения и использовании архивных фондов]

S Contencioso archivístico

CONSERVATION *See* PRESERVATION

CONTACT COPY

A *copy* produced by holding a *sheet* of sensitized material in direct contact with the *original document* or photographic *negative* during exposure.

D Contactadruk

G Kontaktkopie

I Copia a contatto, stampa a contatto

COPIE PAR CONTACT 106

Reproduction obtenue par contact direct entre un *document original* ou son *négatif* photographique et un *papier* traité.

R [Копия, полученная контактным способом]

S Copia por contacto

CONTAINER *See* BOX

CONTINUING VALUE *See* ARCHIVAL VALUE

CONTINUITY FILE *See* CHRONOLOGICAL FILE

CONTRAST

An expression in photography of the relationship between the high and low brightness of a subject, or bet-

CONTRASTE 107

Expression employée dans la terminologie photographique désignant les relations entre les luminosités

(continued)

ween the high and low *density* of a photographic image.

D Contrast

G Kontrast

I Constrasto

forte et faible d'un objet ou entre les densités forte et faible d'une *image* photographique.

R Контрастность

S Contraste

CONVENIENCE FILE *See* OFFICE FILE(S) (2)

COPIER-DUPLICATOR

A device for making single or multiple *copies* of an *original* or another *copy* by photocopying methods without the need for a special *master*.

D Fotokopieerapparaat

G Fotokopierer/-kopiergerät

I Fotocopiatrice, macchina per fotocopie

PHOTOCOPIEUSE 108

Appareil permettant la confection automatique et sans *négatif* inter- médiaire d'une ou de plusieurs *copies* soit d'un *original*, soit d'une *copie* antérieure.

R [Копировальный аппарат]

S Fotocopiadora

COPY

A duplication of the text of an *original document* prepared simul- taneously or separately, usually identified by function or by method of creation. *See also* CARBON COPY: CERTIFICATION (2): CONTACT COPY: ENGROSSED COPY: FACSIMILE: FAIR COPY: FIGURED COPY: LETTERPRESS COPY BOOK: RECORD COPY.

D Kopie

G Kopie, (hand- oder maschinen- schriftliche) Abschrift

I Copia

COPIE 109

Reproduction, simultanée ou non, du texte d'un *document original*, généralement définie par sa fonction ou par son procédé de réalisation. tel que *photocopie, xérographie* ou *carbone. Voir aussi* (58) CARBONE, (174) COPIE AU NET, (177) COPIE FIGURÉE, (106) COPIE PAR CON- TACT, (388) EXEMPLAIRE DE RÉFÉRENCE, (173) FAC-SIMILÉ, (161) GROSSE.

R Копия

S Copia

COPYRIGHT

The right vested by law in the author of a *document*, his heirs or assigns to publish or reproduce

COPYRIGHT, PROPRIÉTÉ LITTÉRAIRE

Droit légal réservant pendant une 110 durée déterminée la publication ou la *reproduction* d'un *document* à

51

(continued)

it or to authorise publication or *reproduction* thereof. Also called literary property right.

D Auteursrecht

G Urheberrecht

I Diritto d'autore, copyright

l'auteur, à ses héritiers ou à leurs ayant droit.

R Авторское право

S Derecho de propiedad intelectual

CORRESPONDENCE

Any form of addressed and written communication sent and received including *letters*, postcards, *memoranda, notes,* telegrams or cables.

D Correspondentie, briefwisseling

G Korrespondenz, Schriftwechsel, Briefwechsel

I Correspondenza, carteggio

CORRESPONDANCE 111

Toute forme de *communication* écrite échangée entre personnes physiques ou morales, reçue *(correspondance passive)* et expédiée *(correspondance active),* notamment les *lettres*, cartes postales, *mémoires, notes, rapports,* télex et télégrammes.

R Переписка

S Correspondencia

CORRESPONDENCE MANAGEMENT

The application of *records management* principles and techniques to *correspondence*. In Canadian usage, treatment of *correspondence*.

D Postbehandeling

G [Rationelle Organisation des Schriftwechsels]

I –

[– – –] 112

Application des techniques de *gestion des documents* à la *correspondance*; au Canada anglophone : traitement de la *correspondance.*

R [Организация переписки]

S –

COUNTERSEAL

A *seal (2)* usually smaller than and distinguished in design from the principal *seal (2)* of an individual user, impressed on the reverse of an impression of the principal *seal (2)* to give added validity and *authentication* to the *document* so validated.

CONTRE-SCEAU 113

Empreinte de *sceau* (1) appliquée au revers d'une autre empreinte de *sceau (1),* de dessin différent et généralement plus petite, conférant au document déjà validé une garantie renforcée d'authenticité.

(continued)

D Tegenzegel, contrazegel

G Rücksiegel, Gegensiegel

I Controsigillo

R –

S Contrasello

CPU *See* CENTRAL PROCESSING UNIT

CUBIC METRE

A unit of measure of the volume of *records (1)* / *archives (1)*, generally used in connection with their *transfer, accessioning* and *disposal*, indicating the volume occupied on average by 9 linear metres or 1500 kilograms of *documents*. One cubic metre equals approximately 35 cubic feet.

D Kubieke meter

G Kubikmeter (als archivische Maßeinheit unüblich)

I Metro cubo

MÈTRE CUBE   114

Unité de volume d'*archives (1)* généralement utilisée lors de transports, de *versements* et d'*éliminations*, et servant à désigner le volume qu'occupent en moyenne 9 mètres linéaires ou 1500 kg d'archives. Le m^3 correspond à 35 pieds cubiques environ.

R –

S Metro cúbico

CULLING *See* WEDDING

CURRENT RECORDS

Records (1) regularly used for the conduct of the current business of an agency, institution or organisation and which, therefore, continue to be maintained in their place of origin. In Canadian usage, active records. *See also* NON-CURRENT RECORDS: SEMI-CURRENT RECORDS.

D Dynamisch archief, lopend archief

G Laufende Akten, Lebende Registratur

I Registratura corrente, archivio corrente, protocollo corrente

ARCHIVES COURANTES   115

Ensemble de *documents d'archives (1)* qui sont d'utilisation habituelle pour l'activité des services, établissements et organismes qui les ont produits et reçus. *Voir aussi* (434) ARCHIVES INTERMÉDIAIRES.

R [Делопроизводственная документация учреждения, используемая в работе]

S Documentos activos

CUSTODY
The basic responsibility for guardianship of *records (1)/archives (1)* based upon their physical possession but not necessarily implying legal title.

D Beheer

G Verwahrung

I Custodia

CONSERVATION (1)   116

Garde physique de *documents d'archives (1)*, impliquant la responsabilité juridique de leur protection, sans nécessairement préjuger de leur propriété.

R Хранение архивных документов

S Custodia, Conservación

CUSTUMAL
A written collection of the customs of, especially, a manor or of a city, town, province or other territorial unit.

D Rechtsboek, wijsdom, costumen

G Rechtsbuch, Statutensammlung

I Raccolta di consuetudini

COUTUMIER   117

Recueil écrit de coutumes, notamment d'une unité territoriale, telle que province, seigneurie ou localité.

R —

S Usatges (Cataluña)

DATA
(1) Facts or instructions represented in a formalised manner, suitable for transmission, interpretation or processing manually or automatically.
(2) Loosely used for *information,* especially in large quantities.

D (1) Data
    (2) Informatie, gegevens

G (1/2) Daten

I (1) Dati
    (2) Informazione

DONNÉE   118

(1) Représentation formalisée de faits ou d'instructions destinée à être traitée par des moyens manuels ou automatiques en vue de sa *communication* ou de son interprétation.
(2) En langage commun: informations en grand nombre.

R (1/2) Данные

S (1/2) Datos

DATA ARCHIVE(S)

An institution or organisation responsible for the *acquisition, preservation* and *communication* of *data (1)* or *(2)* in machine-readable form regardless of *provenance (1)*. *See also* MACHINE-READABLE RECORDS/ARCHIVES.

D Data-archief

G Datenarchiv(e)

I Centro di documentazione automatizzata

ARCHIVES DE DONNÉES INFORMATIQUES 119

Institution ou organisme chargé de centraliser, de conserver et de communiquer des *données (1)* ou *(2)* sous une forme lisible par machine, sans distinction de provenance. Les 'archives de données' ne sont pas synonymes d'*archives lisibles par machine*.

R Архив данных

S Centro de proceso de datos

DATA BANK

A collection of *files (3)* and/or groups of *files (3)* relating to a given subject area and assembled to be made available to various users.

D Databank

G Datenbank

I Banca dei dati

BANQUE DE DONNÉES 120

Collection de *données (1)* et de *dossiers (3)* apparentés relatifs à un domaine défini des connaissances, présentée généralement sous forme lisible par machine et organisée de manière que les *données (1)* originelles ainsi que les *données (2)* nouvellement emmagasinées puissent être repérées et exploitées par recombinaison au moyen d'équipements de *traitement automatique de données*.

R Банк данных

S Banco de datos

DATA BASE

A structured assembly of logically related *data (1)* designed to meet various applications but managed independently of them.

D Database

G Datenbestand, Datenbasis

I Base dei dati

BASE DE DONNÉES 121

Collection organisée de *données (1)*, logiquement reliées entre elles, destinée à répondre aux besoins d'applications diverses et géré indépendamment de chacune d'elles.

R База данных

S Base de datos

DATA PROCESSING *See* AUTOMATIC DATA PROCESSING

DATA RECORD *See* RECORD(S) (2)

DATA SET *See* FILE (3)

DAYBOOK

A *diary, journal,* or other *volume* used for recording one or more types of transactions on a daily basis. Also called waste book.

D Dagboek, journaal

G Tagebuch

I Diario, giornale

JOURNAL COMPTABLE 122

Document plus ou moins spécialisé où sont enregistrés au jour le jour un ou plusieurs types d'opérations dans leur ordre chronologique.

R Журнал, Дневник

S Diario

DAY FILE *See* CHRONOLOGICAL FILE

DEACIDIFICATION

The process by which the *pH value* of *paper documents* is raised to a minimum of 7.0 to assist in their *preservation.* The process is generally used before *hand* or *thermoplastic lamination.* Also referred to as Barrow Process.

D Ontzuren

G Entsäuerung

I Deacidificazione

DÉSACIDIFICATION 123

Procédé par lequel la teneur en acidité des *documents* sur *papier* est diminuée au minimum de 7 % pour en faciliter la *préservation;* le procédé est utilisé en général avant la *lamination thermoplastique.*

R Нейтрализация кислотности бумаги

S Neutralización

DECIMAL CLASSIFICATION

A *classification* using a decimal notation, i.e. including up to ten classes in an array, or series of

CLASSIFICATION DÉCIMALE 124

Système de *classement* reposant systématiquement sur une division en dix parties, appliquée successive-

(continued)

subordinated classes.

D Decimale classificatie

G Dezimalklassifikation, Dezimalgliederung

I Classificazione decimale

ment aux *séries,* aux *sous-séries* et aux subdivisions.

R Десятичная классификация

S Clasificación decimal

DECLASSIFICATION

The removal of all *security class- ification* restrictions on *informa- tion* or *records (1)*. *See also* DOWNGRADE.

D Derubriceren

G Offenlegung von Verschluß- sachen

I Revoca della qualifica di segretezza, declassificazione (military)

[Déclassement]   125

Levée de toute restriction à la *communication* d'un *document (1)* ou à la divulgation de l'information qu'il contient.

R Рассекречивание

S Liberalización

DEED

A *document* under *seal,* in many countries made before a notary public, which, when delivered, gives effect to some legal disposi- tion or agreement between parties. *See also* CHARTER: MUNIMENTS.

D Authentike akte

G Vertragsurkunde

I –

CONTRAT   126

Document muni d'un ou de plusieurs signes de validation établi dans de nombreux pays par devant une autorité publique (notaire ou autre) et qui, une fois délivré, donne effet à une disposition légale ou à un accord entre parties.

R Акт, контракт. Нотариальный акт

S Contrato

DEHUMIDIFICATION

The reduction of the relative humidity of the atmosphere in a storage area by the use of chemical or mechanical methods.

D Droging, ontvochting

G Entfeuchtung

I Deumidificazione

DÉSHUMIDIFICATION   127

Réduction du degré hygrométrique dans les *magasins* au moyen de procédés mécaniques ou chimiques.

R [Снижение относительной влажности в архивохра- нилище]

S Deshumidificación

DENSITY
(1) The opacity of the non-*information* area of an *image*. Optical density is the light-absorbing quality of a photographic *image* (degree of opacity of *film* and blackness of paper *prints*) usually expressed as the logarithm of the opacity.
(2) In *automatic data processing,* the number of *bits* or *characters* that can be stored per unit of dimension of a *medium.* In the case of *magnetic tape*, this is expressed as *bits* per inch (bpi).

D (1) Densiteit
(2) Dichtheid

G (1) Dichte
(2) Speicherdichte

I (1/2) Densità

DENSITÉ   **128**
(1) Dans une *image*, opacité de la surface ne contenant pas d'information, définissant le degré de *contraste* des *épreuves* ou des projections.
(2) En *traitement automatique des données,* nombre d'éléments binaires, de groupes d'éléments binaires ou de *caractères* susceptibles d'être enregistrés par unité de longueur sur un *support;* sur une *bande magnétique,* la densité est exprimée en nombre de rangées par pouce (inch) (r.p.i.).

R (1) Оптическая плотность фона

(2) –

S (1/2) Densidad

DEPARTMENTAL RECORDS/
ARCHIVES
Records (1) /*archives (1)* and/or *archives (2)* of a government department or other administrative agency.

D [Departementaal archief]

G Behördenakten, -archiv(e)

I Registratura, archivio di una amministrazione

ARCHIVES ADMINISTRATIVES   **129**
Archives (1 ou 2) courantes, parfois aussi historiques, d'une entité administrative.

R Документальный фонд, архив учреждения

S Documentos/archivos administrativos

DEPOSIT
(1) The placing of documents in the *custody* of *archives (2)* without transfer of legal title.
(2) The *documents* covered by a single *deposit (1).*
See also ACQUISITION.

D (1/2) Bewaargeving

G (1) Deponierung
(2) Depositum

I (1) Deposito
(2) Deposito, documenti depositati

DÉPÔT   **130**
(1) Transfert de *documents* sous la garde d'un service d'*archives (2)* sans transfert de propriété.
(2) *Documents* ainsi transférés.
Voir aussi (9) ACCROISSEMENT.

R (1) Депонирование документов
(2) Депонированные документы, депозит

S (1/2) Depósito

DEPOSITORY *See* ARCHIVES (3)

DESCRIPTION
The preparation of *finding aids* to facilitate control and consultation of *holdings*.

D Beschrijving
G Verzeichnung
I Inventariazione

[Description] **131**
Élaboration des *instruments de recherche* en vue de faciliter le contrôle et la consultation des *fonds* et *collections*.

R (1) Описание архивных документов
(2)[Подготовка архивных справочников]

S Descripción

DESCRIPTIVE INVENTORY *See* INVENTORY

DESCRIPTIVE LIST
A *finding aid* in the form of a *list* containing brief details of individual *items* generally more detailed than a *class list* (UK). *See also* CATALOGUE: SPECIAL LIST.

D –
G Repertorium
I Inventario analitico

RÉPERTOIRE NUMÉRIQUE DÉTAILLÉ
Instrument de recherche analysant **132** les *articles* d'une manière plus ou moins approfondie selon leur contenu, plus détaillé que le *répertoire numérique*.

R Архивная опись
S Inventario analítico

DESTRUCTION
The *disposal* of *documents* of no further value by *incineration, maceration, pulping* or *shredding*.

D Vernietiging
G Kassation, (Akten)Vernichtung
I Scarto, eliminazione, distruzione

ÉLIMINATION **133**
Destruction de *documents* dénués d'utilité administrative ou archivistique opérée conformément à une réglementation s'il s'agit d'*archives (1)* d'origine publique.

R Уничтожение документов
S Eliminación

DESTRUCTION SCHEDULE *See* RECORDS SCHEDULE

DIARY
A daily written record of events.
See also JOURNAL.

JOURNAL (1) **134**
Enregistrement d'événements jour par jour. *Voir* (252)
JOURNAL (2).

(continued)

D Dagboek

G Tagebuch

I Diario, giornale

R Дневник

S Diario

DIAZO FILM

A type of *film* used in duplicating *microfilm* in which an *image* is produced by the effect of light on diazonium-sensitized materials.

D Diazofilm

G Diazo-Film

I Pellicola diazo, diazo film

FILM DIAZO 135

Type de *film* employé pour la *reproduction* d'une *microforme* résultant de l'action de la lumière sur un *support* recouvert d'une émulsion de colorants diazoïques.

R Диазофильм .

S Película diazo

DIPLOMA

(1) A *charter* issued by a sovereign.
(2) A formal *document* conferring some honour, degree, privilege or licence.

D (1/2) Diploma

G (1/2) Diplom

I (1/2) Diploma

DIPLÔME 136

(1) *Charte* émanant d'un souverain.
(2) *Acte* officiel conférant un honneur, un titre ou un grade.

R (1) Жалованная грамота, диплом.
(2) диплом

S (1/2) Diploma

DIPLOMATIC

The science dealing with the types and elements of *documents.*

D Oorkondenleer, diplomatiek

G Urkundenlehre, Diplomatik; (für die Neuzeit:) Aktenkunde, Formenlehre (neuzeitlichen Schriftguts)

I Diplomatica

DIPLOMATIQUE 137

Discipline ayant pour objet la description et l'explication des types et des formes des *actes* écrits.

R Дипломатика

S Diplomática

DIPLOMATIC ARCHIVES

Archives (1) resulting from the conduct of the foreign affairs of a country.

ARCHIVES DIPLOMATIQUES 138

Archives (1) résultant de l'activité du département ministériel chargé des relations d'un pays avec l'étranger.

D Diplomatieke archieven

G Diplomatische(s) Archiv(e)

I Archivio diplomatico, archivio storico diplomatico

R Дипломатическая докумен-тация

S Archivos diplomáticos

DIRECTIVES MANAGEMENT

The application of *records management* principles and techniques to general instructions, orders or other official issuances.

D —

G Organisation des Vorschriften-wesens

I —

[– – –]   139

Application des principes et des tech-niques de la *gestion des documents* aux instructions et notes de service officiels.

R [Ведение системы организа-ционно-распорядительной документации]

S —

DISASTER PLAN

The policies, procedures, and arrangements intended to be put into effect by an institution, organisation or *archives (2)* in the event of a natural or man-made disaster. *See also* VITAL RECORDS MANAGEMENT.

D Rampenplan

G Katastrophenplan, Notstands-plan(ung)

I Piano di pronto intervento in caso di calamità

[– – –]   140

Partie du plan de protection civile applicable aux *archives (2)* en cas de désastre naturel ou d'origine humaine.

R [План эвакуации документов]

S Plan de emergencia

DISC/DISK *See* FLOPPY DISC/DISK:MAGNETIC DISC/DISK: SOUND RECORDING: VIDEO DISC/DISK

DISINFECTION/DISINFESTATION *See* FUMIGATION

DISKETTE *See* FLOPPY DISC/DISK

DISPLAY CASE

A piece of protective equipment with transparent surfaces for exhibiting *documents*. Also called exhibition case: showcase.

VITRINE   141

Meuble de protection à parois transparentes construit pour exposer des *documents*.

D Vitrine

G (Ausstellungs)Vitrine

I Bacheca

R Витрина

S Vitrina

DISPOSAL

The actions taken with regard to *non-current records* following their *appraisal* and the expiration of their *retention periods* as provided for by legislation, regulation or administrative procedure. Frequently used as synonymous with *destruction*.

D [Separeren] , [Separeren van te vernietigen en van over te bregen semi-statische archief-bescheiden]

G Aussonderung; (Au.:) Skar-tierung

I Scarto

[– – –]   142

Définition du sort à réserver aux *dossiers clos* à l'expiration des délais de *conservation (2)* administrative, en fonction de leur valeur.

R Выделение документов к уничтожению

S Expurgo, tría

DISPOSAL DATE

The date on which the specified *disposal* actions should be initiated as provided in a *records schedule*.

D –

G Aussonderungsdatum, -frist

I –

[Délai de tri]   143

Durée à l'expiration de laquelle le *tri* peut commencer conformément au *règlement de tri*.

R Срок хранения документов

S Fecha de expurgo, fecha de tría

DISPOSAL LIST

A *document* providing one-time only legal authorisation for the *disposal* of the *records (1)* spe-cified therein. *See also* TRANSFER LIST.

D –

G Aussonderungsliste

I Massimario di scarto

VISA D'ÉLIMINATION   144

Liste énumérative de *documents* donnant autorisation légale à leur *élimination*.

R АКТ о выделении докумен-тов к уничтожению

S Lista de expurgo/tría

DISPOSAL MICROFILMING

The use of *microfilm* to save or recover storage space and equipment and the substitution of the *microfilms* for the *originals* which are destroyed. Also called space-saving or substitution microfilming. *See also* PRESERVATION MICROFILMING.

D Substitutieverfilming

G Ersatzverfilmung

I Microfilmatura di sostituzione

MICROFILMAGE DE SUBSTITUTION 145

Établissement de *microfilm* de *documents originaux* ultérieurement détruits, en vue de réutiliser la place et les équipements ainsi libérés.

R [Использование микрофиль-мов для экономии площади архивохранилищ и замены утраченных оригиналов]

S Microfilmación de sustitución

DISPOSAL SCHEDULE *See* RECORDS SCHEDULE

DISPOSITION *See* DISPOSAL

DOCUMENT

(1) A combination of a *medium* and the *information* recorded on or in it, which may be used as evidence or for consultation.
(2) A single archival, *record* or *manuscript item.*

D (1) Document
(2) Stuk

G (1) Dokument, Schriftstück
(2) Dokument

I (1) Documento
(2) Documento (non comprende il manoscritto)

DOCUMENT 146

(1) Ensemble constitué par un *support* et par l'information qu'il porte, utilisable à des fins de consultation ou comme preuve.
(2) [Pièce d'*archives (1)* ou *manuscrit.*]

R (1/2) Документ, Архивный документ

S (1/2) Documento

DOCUMENT CASE

A container for the *flat-filing* of *documents*. Also known as a clam shell case (US) or solander clase (UK).

D Portefeuille

G Klappkarton

I Cartella

PORTEFEUILLE 147

Carton à couvercle destiné à la *conservation à plat* de *documents.*

R Коробка для документов

S Carpeta

DOCUMENTARY PUBLICATION

The publication, in whatever form, of authentic texts and other *documents* with appropriate description and critical annotation.

D Tekstuitgave, bronnenpublikatie

G Dokumenten-, Aktenpublikation

I Edizione critica di fonti documentarie

PUBLICATION DE DOCUMENTS 148

Publication de tout type de *documents d'archives* accompagnée d'un apparat descriptif, explicatif et critique.

R документальная публикация

S Edición de textos

DOCUMENTATION

(1) The organisation and processing of *documents* or *data (1)* including location, identification, *acquisition*, analysis, storage, retrieval, presentation and circulation for the *information* of *users*.
(2) In *machine-readable records/archives,* an organised series of descriptive *documents (1)* explaining the *operating system* and *software* necessary to use and maintain a *file (2)* and the arrangement, content and coding of the *data (1)* which it contains.

D (1/2) Documentatie

G (1/2) Dokumentation

I (1) Documentazione
(2) Documentazione operativa

DOCUMENTATION 149

(1) Collecte méthodique et traitement de *documents* et de *données (1)* opérés pour l'information des utilisateurs, comprenant notamment la localisation, l'identification, l'acquisition, l'analyse, la *conservation,* le repérage et la diffusion.
(2) Dans les *archives informatiques,* ensemble organisé de *documents* (1) descriptifs du *système d'exploitation* et du *logiciel,* nécessaires à l'utilisation d'un *fichier* et au codage des *données (1)* que ce *dossier (2)* contient.

R (1) —

(2) [Документация]

S (1/2) Documentación

DONATION *See* GIFT

DONOR

The source from which a *gift* originates.

D Schenker

G Schenker, Stifter

I Donatore

DONATEUR 150

Personne physique ou morale ayant effectué un *don* ou une dation d'*archives (1).*

R Даритель документов

S Donante

DOSSIER *See* CASE PAPERS/FILES

DOUBLE SHELVING
  The placing of *items* or containers
  behind each other on the same *shelf.*

D –
G Doppelreihige Aufstellung
  (von Akten oder Büchern)
I Doppiafila

[– – –]   151
  Rangement des *articles* ou des *cartons*
  en double file sur la même *tablette*;
  rangement de *cartons* au-dessus l'un
  de l'autre sur la même *tablette* (B, US.)

R [Размещение коробок в
  два ряда на полке]
S Instalación en doble hilera

DOWNGRADE
  To reduce the level of *security*
  classification of specified
  information/records (1). See also
  DECLASSIFICATION.

D Derubriceren
G Herabstufen von Verschlußsachen
I –

[Rétrogradation]   152
  Passage à un échelon inférieur dans
  les degrés du classement de sécurité.

R Рассекречивание
S Liberar

DRAFT
  (1) A rough or preliminary
  form of a *document*, sometimes
  retained as evidence.
  (2) A written order directing the
  payment of money.

D (1) Concept
  (2) Mandaat
G (1) Entwurf, Konzept
  (2) Zahlungsanweisung
I (1) Prima stesura, prima
      bozza, prima minuta,
      brogliaccio
  (2) Mandato di pagamento

BROUILLON   153
  (1) Libellé préliminaire d'un écrit,
  mis en forme ou non, ou première
  rédaction conservée à titre de
  témoignage.
  (2) [Ordre écrit de paiement(U.K.)]

R (1) Черновик, проект
      документа
S (1) Borrador, minuta
  (2) Orden de pago, libranza

DRAWING *See* TECHNICAL DRAWING

DRY SILVER PROCESS
  A silver halide copying process in
  which the latent *image* is made
  visible by the application of heat
  rather than of chemicals.

PROCÉDÉ ARGENTIQUE   154
  Procédé de *copie* aux sels d'argent
  où l'*image* latente devient visible
  sous l'action de la chaleur.

(continued)

D Zilverhalide procédé

G Trockensilberverfahren,
Dry-Silber-Prozeß

I Procedimento agli alogenuri
d'argento

R —

S Procesado en seco

DUMMY
A card, *sheet* or other indicator
placed on or near the place where
an *item* is normally stored to
denote its removal.

D [Vlag]

G Stellvertreter, Retent

I Scheda di richiamo

FANTÔME   155
Fiche cartonnée ou non, cotée et
datée, mise à la place d'un *article*
pendant la durée de son déplacement. *Voir* (73,2) FICHE DE
DÉPLACEMENT.

R Карта – заместитель еди-
ницы хранения

S Testigo, momio

DUPLICATE *See* COPY

ECCLESIASTICAL ARCHIVES *See* CHURCH ARCHIVES

EDITING *See* HISTORICAL EDITING

EDUCATION(AL) SERVICE
The activities of *archives (2)*
intended to encourage and
further the use of its *holdings*
in the field of education at
all levels.

D Educatieve dienstverlening

G Archivpädagogische Arbeit,
Zusammenarbeit mit der
Schule

I Servizio educativo

SERVICE ÉDUCATIF   156
Dans un service d'*archives (2)*,
fonction d'enseignement destinée
à élargir la connaissance des
archives (1) et initier le public
notamment scolaire à leur exploitation.

R [Информационная деятель-
ность архивов в учебно-
воспитательных целях]

S Servicio educativo

ELECTRONIC DATA PROCESSING *See* AUTOMATIC DATA PROCESSING

ELECTROSTATIC PROCESS
A direct, dry *reproduction* process creating *copies* on ordinary *paper* in an automatic machine using electrical photoconductivity.

D Elektrostatisch kopieerprocédé

G Elektrostatisches Kopierverfahren

I Xerografia

XÉROGRAPHIE 157
Procédé de *reproduction* direct et à sec sur *papier* ordinaire par un appareil utilisant la photoconductibilité électrique.

R Ксерография

S Procedimiento electroestático, Xerografía

ELIMINATION *See* DESTRUCTION

EMULSION
A gelatinous coating of chemicals which react to radiant energy on a transparent base which creates a latent *image* upon exposure.

D Emulsie

G Emulsion, Schicht

I Emulsione

ÉMULSION 158
Couche de gélatine recouvrant un *film* transparent sur laquelle l'exposition provoque la formation de l'*image* latente.

R эмульсионный слой

S Emulsión

ENCAPSULATION
The encasing of a *document* in a plastic *envelope* of which the edges are then sealed.

D Insealen, inkapselen

G Einschweißen

I Conservazione dei documenti in cartelle di plasticata sigillate

[Conservation en pochettes closes] 159
Mode de protection de *documents* entre deux surfaces de plastique transparent aux bords soudés.

R [Хранение документов в классерах, в джекетах]

S Encapsulado

ENDORSEMENT
A *note*, title, *signature (1)*, etc. written on the back of a *document*.

D Endorsement

G Rückvermerk, Dorsualvermerk (-signatur)

I Nota dorsale

MENTION DORSALE 160
Indications brèves, telles que *note, cote,* analyse, portées au verso d'un *document*.

R Индоссамент. пометки, подписи на обороте документа

S Notas dorsales

ENGROSSED COPY
The final version of a *document,*
drawn up in due form.

D Grosse, expeditie

G Ausfertigung, Mundum

I Originale, bella copia, grossa,
copia a buono (*obsolete*)

GROSSE, EXPÉDITION   **161**
Acte rédigé par un notaire selon les
formes prescrites et dans les termes
définitifs sous lesquels il doit être
délivré à son destinataire.

R Беловик

S Original

ENGROSSMENT
(1) The preparation of an
engrossed copy.
(2) An *engrossed copy.*

D (1) Grosseren
   (2) Grosse

G (1/2) Ausfertigung

I (1) Redazione dell' origi-
   nale/della bella copia/
   della grossa

[– – –]   **162**
(1) Action de rédiger une *grosse.*
(2) Grosse.

R (1) Переписывание набело
   (2) Беловик

S (1) Puesta en limpio
   (2) Original

ENLARGEMENT
A *reproduction* larger than the
original or the intermediate used
to make the *reproduction.*

D Vergroting

G Vergrößerung

I Ingrandimento

AGRANDISSEMENT   **163**
Copie d'un *document* avec des
dimensions agrandies.

R [Увеличение размеров копий при репродуцировании]

S Ampliación

ENLARGEMENT RATIO *See* MAGNIFICATION

ENLARGER-PRINTER
An optical device for producing
enlargements, incorporating
processing facilities for the
rapid production of *hard copy,*
usually under conditions of
room lighting.

AGRANDISSEUR IMPRIMANT   **164**
Appareil optique à développeuse
incorporée produisant rapidement
des *agrandissements* sur *papier,*
généralement dans des conditions
d'éclairage normal.

D Vergroter

G Vergrößerungs-Druckgerät

I Ingraditore-stampatore

R Копировальный аппарат для
получения увеличенных
копий

S Ampliadora

ENROLMENT

The entering of a *copy* of a
document in the *records (1)*
of a court of record (UK).

[– – –]   165

Enregistrement d'une *copie* de
document par une institution
judiciaire (UK.)

D [Op de rol plaatsen]

G Registrierung, Eintragung (in
ein gerichtliches Register)

I Registrazione giudiziaria

R [Запись текста документа
в актовой книге]

S Registro

ENTRY

(1) The recording in a list, *journal,
register,* etc. of a *document* or
transaction.
(2) An *item* thus recorded.
(3) The unit of description in a
finding aid.

(1) ANALYSE   166

Description d'une *pièce,* d'un
dossier ou d'un groupe de *dossiers*
dans un *instrument de recherche.*
(2) *Pièce, dossier* ou groupe de *dossiers*
ainsi décrit.
(3) Unité de description dans un
instrument de recherche.
(4) ENREGISTREMENT
Transcription ou mention plus ou
moins systématique, officielle ou
non, de *données (2)* dans un
registre.

D (1) Boeken, inschrijven
(2) Post
(3) Beschrijving

G (1/2/3) Eintrag

I (1) Registrazione
(2) Documento registrato
(3) Unità archivistica di
inventariazione

R (3) Описательная статья в
архивном справочнике

S (1) Asiento

ENVELOPE

A folded container for *letters*
or other *documents.*

ENVELOPPE   167

Feuille de *papier* pliée et collée en
forme de poche, munie ou non de
bords gommés assurant une fermeture
et destinée à contenir une *lettre* ou
un ensemble de *pièces.*

(continued)

D Envelop, enveloppe

G Umschlag

I Busta

R Конверт

S Sobre

EPHEMERA

Informal *documents* of transitory value, sometimes preserved as samples or specimens.

D Efemeer materiaal

G Weglegesachen

I Documento di valore contingente

[– – –]   168

Documents informels de valeur temporaire, parfois conservés à titre d'échantillon

R [документы временного хранения]

S Documento efímeros

ESTATE ARCHIVES *See* FAMILY (AND ESTATE) ARCHIVES

ESTRAY

A *document* not in the possession of its legal custodian (US).
See also ALIENATION.

D Afgedwaald stuk

G [Entfremdetes Dokument]

I –

[– – –]   169

Document qui n'est pas en possession de son conservateur légal.

R Бесхозные документы

S –

ESTREAT *See* EXTRACT (2)

EVALUATION *See* APPRAISAL

EVIDENTIAL VALUE

The value of *records (1)/archives (1)* of an institution or organisation in providing evidence of its origins, structure, functions, procedures and significant transactions as distinct from *informational value. See also* ADMINISTRATIVE VALUE: FISCAL VALUE: LEGAL VALUE.

(1) VALEUR PROBATOIRE   170

Valeur intrinsèque des *documents d'archives (1)* qui leur permet de servir de preuve.

(2) [Valeur institutionelle]

Valeur inhérente à un *fonds d'archives (1)* qui permet d'établir l'origine, la structure, la compétence et le fonctionnement caractérisant l'institution créatrice; s'oppose à 'informational value'.

(continued)

D Bewijskracht

G Beweiswert

I Valore di prova, valore
probatorio

R [Доказательная ценность
документа]

S Valor probatorio

EXHIBITION

The display of *original documents*
or *copies* thereof for educational
and cultural purposes. *See also*
ARCHIVAL MUSEUM.

D Tentoonstelling

G Ausstellung

I Mostra

EXPOSITION D'ARCHIVES 171

Présentation temporaire de *documents
d'archives (1)* ou de leur *reproduction*
à des fins culturelles ou éducatives.
Voir aussi (31) MUSÉE D'ARCHIVES.

R Выставка

S Exposición

EXHIBITION CASE *See* DISPLAY CASE

EXPOSURE *See* FRAME

EXTENSION SERVICE *See* OUTREACH PROGRAMME

EXTRACT

(1) A *copy* of part of the text
of a *document*.
(2) An authentic *copy* of an
entry (2) especially used for
entries in *register(s)*.

D (1) Uittreksel
(2) Authentiek uittreksel

G (1) Auszug, Teilabschrift
(2) Auszug, Extrakt (Extractus
protocolli)

I (1) Estratto
(2) Estratto autenticato

EXTRAIT 172

(1) *Copie* partielle d'un *document*
établie dans un but défini.
(2) [*Copie* authentique d'une
inscription ou d'une notice dans
un *document original*.]

R (1) Выписка из документа.
(2) экстракт

S (1/2) Extracto

FACILITATIVE RECORDS *See* HOUSKEEPING RECORDS (US)

FACSIMILE
A *reproduction*, similar in size and
appearance, of a *document*.

D Facsimile

G Faksimile

I Facsimile

FAIR COPY
An exact *copy* of a *document*
incorporating all final textual
corrections and revisions. *See
also* ENGROSSED COPY.

D Minuut

G Reinkopie

I Minuta definitiva

FAMILY (AND ESTATE) ARCHIVES
Archives (1) and/or *archives (2)*
of one or more related families
and/or the individual members
thereof relating to their private
and public affairs and to the administration of their estates. Also called
patrimonial archives.

D Familie- (en huis)archief

G Familien- (Herrschafts- und
Guts-) Archiv(e)

I Archivi di famiglia

FIELD-BOOK
A *volume* which identifies, by
numbers referring to parcels of
land delineated on a *map*, all lands
within a given geographical area
with the names of their owners and,
usually, their extent and occupiers.
See also SURVEY.

D Legger

G Flurbuch, Kataster

I Brogliardo (di castato
particellare)

FAC-SIMILÉ 173
Reproduction d'un *document* dans
son apparence et sa forme.

R Факсимиле

S Facsímil

COPIE AU NET 174
Copie d'un *document* après toutes
les révisions et corrections finales
du texte. *Voir aussi* (161) GROSSE.

R Беловик

S Copia literal

ARCHIVES DE FAMILLES 175
Archives (1 ou 2) d'une ou de
plusieurs familles alliées et de leurs
membres, relatives à leurs affaires
privées, notamment la gestion des
biens et, éventuellement, à leurs
activités publiques.

R Семейный и вотчинный
архивный фонд

S Archivos familiares

CADASTRE 176
Registre contenant la liste numérotée
de toutes les parcelles situées dans un
espace géographique donné (seigneurie,
commune), avec leur *plan*, leur super-
ficie et les noms des propriétaires ou
des occupants. *Voir aussi* (467)
ENQUÊTE CADASTRALE (2).

R Земельный кадастр

S Catastro

FIGURED COPY

An exact *copy* of a *document* of earlier date incorporated in the text of a later *document*, usually prepared for legal purposes, purporting to reproduce accurately the handwriting and form of the *original* (UK).

D Copie figurée

G Nachzeichnung

I Copia imitativa (non inserta in altro documento); inserto (non imitativo)

COPIE FIGURÉE 177

(1) *Copie* d'un *document*, reproduisant ses caractéristiques matérielles.
(2) [*Copie* exacte d'un *document* incorporée dans le texte d'un *document* ultérieur, généralement établie à des fins légales et se proposant d'en reproduire fidèlement le graphisme et la forme (UK).]

R Факсимильная копия

S Copia figurada

FILE

(1) An organised unit (*folder, volume*, etc.) of *documents* grouped together either for current use or in the process of archival *arrangement*.
(2) A series of *files (1)* (US).
(3) In *machine-readable records/ archives*, two or more *records(2)* of indentical layout treated as a unit. The unit is larger than a *record (2)* but smaller than a data system, and is also known as a data set or file set.

D (1) Bundel, dossier
   (2) –
   (3) Bestand

G (1) Aktenband, -heft
   (2) Aktenserie, -gruppe, Ablage
   (3) Datei

I (1) Unità archivistica
   (2) Gruppo di unità archivistica
   (3) File, unità seriale di dati

DOSSIER 178

(1) Ensemble de *documents* constitué soit organiquement par l'administration d'origine, soit par regroupement lors du *classement* aùx *archives (2)*.
(2) [Série de *dossiers (1)*, U.S.]
(3) Dans les *archives informatiques*, deux ou plusieurs *données (1)* traitées comme un *article*.

R (1) Дело
   (3) Файл

S (1) Expediente
   (2) Serie de expedientes
   (3) Fichero

FILE BREAK

A convenient point within a *filing plan/system* (end of a letter of the alphabet, end of year or month, etc) at which individual *files (1)* are separated for purposes of *appraisal, scheduling,* and *disposal*.

[– – –] 179

Critère alphabétique, géographique, temporel à partir duquel un *plan de classement* sépare les *dossiers* à conserver intégralement de ceux qui sont à trier et à éliminer.

(continued)

D [Splitsing van dossiers]
G Einschnitt
I –

R –
S Corte de serie

FILE COPY *See* RECORD COPY

FILE COVER *See* FOLDER

FILE SET *See* FILE (3)

FILE UNIT *See* FILE (1)

FILES
A collective term frequently applied to part or all the *records (1)* of an agency.

D Archief

G Akten

I Gruppo di registratura di un' amministrazione, archivio generale di deposito

[Fonds d'archives courantes]   **180**
Terme collectif appliqué à une partie ou à l'ensemble des *archives courantes* d'une institution.

R Дела, документальный фонд

S Fondo

FILES ADMINISTRATION/MANAGEMENT
The application of *records management* principles and techniques to *filing plans/systems* and practices.

D [Administratief beheer van dynamische en semistatische archiefbescheiden]

G Aktenverwaltung, Aktenorganisation

I –

[– – –]   **181**
Application des principes et des techniques de *gestion des documents* au *classement* d'*archives (1)*.

R [Организация разработки и применения номенклатур дел]

S Organización de fondos de archivos

FILING
The placing of *documents* in a predetermined location according to a *filing plan/system*.

CLASSEMENT (2)   **182**
Rangement de *documents* selon un plan préétabli de répartition.

74

D Klasseren

G (Akten)Ablage

I Collocazione

R Формирование дел

S Colocación

FILING PLAN/SYSTEM

A predetermined *classification plan* for the physical *arrangement*, storage and retrieval of *files (1)*, usually identified by the type of symbols used e.g. alphabetical, numerical, alpha-numerical, decimal. *See also* STANDARDIZED FILING PLAN/SYSTEM.

D Ordeningsplan

G Aktenplan

I Piano di disposizione dei documenti

[Plan de rangement]   183

Plan préétabli permettant de classer, emmagasiner et retrouver des *dossiers (1)*, généralement identifiés par une *cote*.

R Номенклатура дел

S Plan de organización de fondos

FILM

A flexible sheet or strip of transparent plastic upon which *images* can be recorded. *See also* DIAZO FILM: MICROFILM: SILVER HALIDE FILM: VESICULAR FILM.

D Film

G Film

I Pellicola, film

FILM   184

Feuille ou bande de plastique flexible capable de fixer des *images*. *Voir aussi* (298) MICROFILM, (444) FILM ARGENTIQUE, (493) FILM VÉSICULAIRE.

R Фотопленка, кинопленка

S Película

FILM ARCHIVES

(1) *Archives (1)* in the form of *motion pictures* with related *textual records/archives*.
(2) An institution responsible for the *acquisition, preservation* and *communication* of *motion pictures* and related materials irrespective of their *provenance (1)* and/or archival character. *See also* AUDIO VISUAL ARCHIVES.

(1) ARCHIVES CINÉMATOGRAPHI-   185
QUES
Archives (1) constituées de *films cinématographiques* et des *documents* s'y rapportant.
(2) CINÉMATHÈQUE
Organisme chargé de la *collecte,* de la *conservation* et de la *communication* de *films cinématographiques* et de *documents* annexes, indépendamment de leur *provenance* ou de leur *valeur archivistique*.

D (1/2) Filmarchief
G (1/2) Filmarchiv(e)
I (1) Archivio cinematografico
   (2) Cineteca

R (1) Кинодокументы
   (2) Архив кинодокументов
S (1) –
   (2) Filmateca

FILM FRAME See FRAME

FILM JACKET See MICROFILM JACKET

FILM STRIP
A short length of *film* carrying
a number of photographic
images.

D Filmstrook

G Filmstreifen

I Striscia di fotogrammi

[– – –]   186
Juxtaposition sur un *film* de clichés
isolés utilisés en projection comme
images fixes.

R Фотодокумент, диафильм
S Tira

FINDING AID
A *document*, published or
unpublished, listing or describing
a body of *record (1)/archives (1)*
thereby establishing administrative and intellectual control over
them by a *records centre/archi-
ves (2)*, making them more
readily accessible and compre-
hensible to the *user*. Basic finding
aids include *guides, inventories,
catalogues, calendars, lists, indexes,
location indexes/registers* and, for
*machine-readable records/archives,
software documentation.* Also called
means of reference.

D Toegang

G Findbehelf, Findbuch

I Mezzo di corredo, strumento
di ricerca

INSTRUMENT DE RECHERCHE   187
Document, imprimé ou non, énumérant
ou décrivant un ensemble de *pièces
d'archives (1)* de manière à les faire
connaître aux chercheurs scientifiques
et administratifs. Les instruments de
recherche fondamentaux comprennent
les *guides, inventaires, catalogues,
regestes, répertoires, index, registres
des emplacements*, et, pour les
archives lisibles par machine, la documentation logicielle.

R Архивный справочник

S Instrumento de trabajo,
Instrumento de consulta

FIRE DETECTION SYSTEM
A system for detecting the outbreak of a fire in its earliest

SYSTÈME DE DÉTECTION D'INCENDIE 18
Système de détection des premiers
signes de feu au moyen d'un détecteur

stages by means of electronic detector heads activated by smoke, rise in temperature or by changes in the ionisation of the atmosphere. Frequently linked to a *fire extinguishing system.*

D Branddetectiesysteem

G Feuermeldeanlage

I Impianto di allarme antincendio

électronique sensible à la fumée, à l'accroissement de la température ou au changement d'ionisation de l'atmosphère.

R Детекторная автоматичес-кая система пожарной защиты

S Sistema de detección de incendios

FIRE EXTINGUISHING SYSTEM

A system for extinguishing a fire by manual or automatic means. Automatic systems are usually linked to a *fire detection system* and operated once that system gives warning of an outbreak of fire. Manual extinguishing may be by water, foam, sand or powder: automatic systems may use water but increasingly use gases e.g. carbon dioxide or halogen. *See also* SPRINKLER SYSTEM.

D Brandblussysteem

G Feuerlöschanlage

I Impianto di estinzione di incendio

SYSTÈME D'EXTINCTION D'INCENDIE 189

Système d'extinction de feu par des moyens manuels ou automatiques. Les moyens manuels emploient l'eau, la mousse, le sable ou la poudre. Les moyens automatiques sont couplés à un *système de détection* d'incendie et se déclanchent dès que l'alerte au feu est donnée; ils emploient l'eau, de plus en plus souvent des gaz, comme le gaz carbonique. *Voir* (453) SPRINK-LER.

R Система пожарной защиты

S Sistema de extinción de incendios

FISCAL VALUE

The value of *records (1)/archives (1)* for the conduct of current or future financial or fiscal business and/or as evidence thereof. *See also* ADMINISTRATIVE VALUE: LEGAL VALUE.

D [Boekhoudkundige waarde]

G [Fiskalischer Wert]

I Validità amministrativa nel settore fiscale

[Valeur fiscale]   190

Valeur que détiennent les *archives (1)* pour la gestion d'affaires financières ou fiscales présentes ou avenir.

R [Практическая ценность финансовой документации]

S Valor fiscal

FLAT-BED CAMERA *See* PLANETARY CAMERA

FLAT-FILING

The placing of *records (1)*/ *archives (1)* whether bound or in containers in a position parallel to the *shelf*. Also called horizontal filing.

D Liggende berging, horizontale berging

G Liegende Aufbewahrung/ Ablage

I Disposizione orizzontale dei documenti sulla scaffalatura

CONSERVATION À PLAT   191

Mode de *conservation* horizontale des *documents*.

R Горизонтальное хранение документов

S Instalación horizontal

FLATTENING

The process of restoring to a flat condition, after *humidification* if they are in a brittle state, *documents* which have been folded, rolled or otherwise in need of such treatment by the application of pressure.

D Vlakken

G Glätten

I Spianamento

MISE À PLAT   192

Procédé de *restauration* consistant à aplatir à la pression des *documents* mal pliés, roulés, gondolés ou froissés, après *humidification* préalable s'ils sont fragiles ou cassants.

R Разглаживание, отпрессовка документов

S Planchado

FLOPPY DISC/DISK

A flexible *magnetic disc/disk* revolving within a protective cover. Also called diskette.

D Floppy disk

G Floppy Disk

I Dischetto magnetico flessibile, floppy disk

MINIDISQUE / DISQUE SOUPLE   193

Disque magnétique flexible tournant muni d'une couverture de protection.

R Гибкий диск

S Disquete, disco flexible

FOLDER

(1) A folded *sheet (1)* of card-board or heavy *paper* serving as a cover for a number of *documents*.
(2) A type of *file (1)*.

D (1) Map
   (2) [Dossier] omslag

CHEMISE   194

(1) Feuille de *papier* fort ou de carton mince pliée en deux servant à isoler et à conserver des *documents*.
(2) [Type de *dossier (1)*.]

R (1) Обложка для докумен- тов
   (2) Дело

(continued)

G (1) (Akten)Deckel
(2) Aktenband, -heft

I (1) Copertina, camicia,
carpetta
(2) Fascicolo

S (1) Camisa, carpetilla
(2) Carpetilla

FOLIATION

(1) The act of *numbering* the
folios (1) of a *document* as
distinct from numbering *pages*,
i.e. *pagination*.
(2) The result of this action.

D (1/2) Foliëring

G (1/2) Foliierung, Blattzählung

I (1/2) Cartolazione, foliazione

FOLIOTAGE 195

(1) Action de numéroter le recto
des *feuillets (1)* d'un *document*, par
opposition à la *pagination*,
numérotation du recto et du verso.
(2) Résultat de cette opération.

R (1/2) Нумерация листов

S (1/2) Foliación

FOLIO

(1) A *leaf* of *paper* or *parchment*
usually folded and numbered
only on the front.
(2) The number assigned to a
leaf.
(3) A *volume* made up of *sheets*
folded once; hence, loosely, a
volume of large dimensions.

D (1/2/3) Folio

G (1) (Doppel)Blatt
(2) Blattnummer
(3) Folioband

I (1) Foglio, carta
(2) Numero
(3) in-folio

(1) FEUILLET (1) 196

Feuille de *papier* ou de *parchemin*,
numérotée seulement au recto.
(2) [Numéro donné à un *feuillet*.]
(3) VOLUME IN-FOLIO
Volume formé de feuilles qui ne
sont pliées qu'une fois; par extension,
volume de grandes dimensions.

R (1) [Лист документа, нумеруемый с лицевой стороны]
(2) Номер листа
(3) Том -фолио, фолиант

S (1/2) Folio
(3) In-folio

FONDS

The total body of *records (1)/*
archives (1) accumulated by a
particular individual, institution
or organisation in the exercise of
its activities and functions. *See
also* ARCHIVE GROUP: RECORD
GROUP: STATE ARCHIVAL
FONDS.

FONDS D'ARCHIVES 197

Ensemble des *documents d'archi-*
ves (1) de toute nature réunis par
une personne physique ou morale
ou une institution dans l'exercice de
ses activités ou de ses fonctions.
Ce terme s'oppose à *collection*.
Voir (30) SERIE (1).

(continued)

D Archief

G Fond, Provenienzbestand

I Fondo, archivio

R Фонд

S Fondo

FORGERY

A *document* falsified wholly or in part in content or form with intention to deceive through its acceptance as an *original*.

D Falsum, vervalsing

G Fälschung

I Falso

FAUX 198

Document (1) altéré partiellement ou en entier dans sa forme ou son contenu, avec l'intention frauduleuse de le faire passer pour un *original*.

R Фальсификат, Подложный документ

S Documento falso

FORM

(1) A *document,* printed or otherwise produced, with predesignated spaces for the recording of specified *information.*
(2) A *document* intended to serve as a model.

D (1/2) Formulier

G (1/2) Formular

I (1) Modulo, modulario
(2) Modello

(1) FORMULAIRE (1) 199

Document produit en nombre par impression ou autre procédé, présentant des espaces à remplir par des informations ultérieurement fournies par l'utilisateur.
(2) MODÈLE
Document servant d'exemple type à imiter.

R (1) Форма, бланк документа
(2) Образец документа

S (1) Formulario, modelo
(2) Modelo

FORMAT

In *automatic data processing*, the arrangement of *data (1)*.

D Indeling

G Format

I Formato

FORMAT 200

Dans le *traitement automatique des données,* disposition définie de *données (1)* sur un *support*.

R Формат

S Formato

FORMS MANAGEMENT

The application of *records management* principles and techniques to the design, construction, produc-

[− − −] 201

Application à l'élaboration, à la production et à l'emploi de *formulaires* des principes et des

80

(continued)

tion, logistics, maintenance, and
use of *forms (1)* (US).

D Formulierenbeheer

G Organisation des Vordruck-
wesens

I −

techniques de la *gestion des
documents.*

R [Совершенствврвание форм
документации]

S Normalización de modelos

FORMULARY

A volume containing *forms (2)*.

D Formulierboek

G Formelbuch, Formularbuch

I Formulario

FORMULAIRE (2)   202

Recueil de formules.

R [Альбом форм документов]

S Formulario

FOXING

The discolaration of *paper*
by brownish stains.

D Roestvlekken

G Stockflecken

I Inbrunimento

ROUSSEUR   203

Tache brunâtre causée au *papier*
par l'humidité.

R Отбеливание бумаги

S Moteado

FRAME

The area of a photographic *film*
exposed to light in a camera during
one *exposure.*

D Beeld

G Bildfeld, Aufnahme

I Area del fotogramma

VUE   204

Surface d'un *film* photographique
soumise à l'action de la lumière pendant
l'exposition.

R Кадр

S Campo de imagen, marco

FRAMING

The reinforcement of the damaged
edges of a *sheet* of *paper* with
repair *paper* or other material
from which the central part covering the text has been removed.
Also called inlaying: window
repair.

D [Aanbrengen van een kader]

G [Randeinbettung]

I Bordatura

BORDAGE   205

Mode de *restauration* de *documents*
aux bords endommagés à l'aide de
papier ou autres matériaux de
renforcement.

R [Закрепление разрушенных
краев листа документа]

S Enmarcado

FREEZE DRYING

The treatment of water-soaked *documents* by quick-freezing and subsequent drying under high vacuum at gradually rising temperatures. *See also* VACUUM DRYING.

D Vriesdrogen

G Gefriertrocknung

I Essiccamento con congelamento sotto vuoto

SÉCHAGE À FROID 206

Traitement de *documents* imbibés d'eau par congélation rapide puis séchage sous vide à une température s'élevant graduellement.

R Просушивание документов

S Liofilización

FUGITIVE ARCHIVES *See* REMOVED ARCHIVES

FUMIGATION

The process of exposing *documents,* usually in a vacuum or other airtight chamber, to gas or vapour to destroy insects, mildew or other forms of life that may endanger them. Also referred to as disinfection/disinfestation.

D Ontsmetting

G Begasung

I Disinfestazione (insects, mildew, etc); disinfezione (microorganisms)

DÉSINFECTION 207

Exposition de *documents* à des vapeurs chimiques sous vide, pour détruire les différentes formes de vie animale et végétale qui attaquent leur intégrité.

R Фумигация, дезинфекция

S Fumigación

FUMIGATION CHAMBER

A vacuum or other airtight chamber used for the *fumigation* of *documents.*

D Ontsmettingskast

G Begasungsschrank, -kammer

I Cella di disinfestazione o di disinfezione

AUTOCLAVE 208

Appareil à fermeture hermétique destiné à désinfecter et à stériliser des *documents d'archives,* notamment avant leur *restauration,* parfois lors de leur entrée aux *archives (2).*

R Дезинфекционная камера

S Cámara de fumigación

FUNCTIONAL ARRANGEMENT *See* ARRANGEMENT

FUNCTIONAL PERTINENCE *See* FUNCTIONAL PROVENANCE

FUNCTIONAL PROVENANCE

The concept that, with a transfer of functions from one authority to another as a result of political or administrative change, relevant *records (1)* or *copies* thereof are also transferred to ensure administrative continuity. Also referred to as functional pertinence.

D Successiebeginsel

G Funktionale Provenienz

I Provenienza funzionale

[– – –]   209

Concept selon lequel, lorsqu'il y a transfert de fonctions d'une autorité à une autre à la suite de changements politiques ou administratifs, les *documents* les concernant ou leurs *copies* doivent être transférés, afin d'assurer la continuité administrative; appelé parfois 'pertinence fonction'.

R [Преемственность в наследовании учреждением – правопреемником документов при административных и политических изменениях]

S Procedencia funcional

GENEALOGY

The science of family relationships.

D Genealogie, geslachtkunde

G Genealogie, Familienforschung

I Genealogia

GÉNÉALOGIE   210

Science cherchant à découvrir l'origine et la filiation des familles.

R Генеалогия

S Genealogía

GENERAL INDEX

An *index* giving *access* to one or more bodies of material or to the totality of *holdings* of a *records centre/archives (2)*.

D Generale index

G Generalindex, -kartei

I Indice generale, repertorio generale

INDEX GÉNÉRAL   211

Index permettant d'accéder au contenu d'un *fonds,* d'un groupe de *fonds* ou de l'ensemble des *documents* d'un service d'*archives (2)*.

R (1)[Общий указатель]
(2)[Архивный каталог]

S Indice general

GENERAL RECORD GROUP

A *record group* comprising the *records (1)* of the office of the head of an organisationally complex agency and the *records (1)* of other units of the agency concerned with matters common to the entire agency (US). *See also* COLLECTIVE RECORD GROUP.

ARCHIVES DE CABINET   212

Fonds comprenant les *documents (1)* d'un ministre ou d'un haut fonctionnaire et de leurs collaborateurs immédiats reçus ou élaborés dans l'exercice de leurs fonctions.

(continued)

D [Centraal archief]

G [Zentralaktenbestand]

I Archivio generale di un' amministrazione

R [Объединенный архивный фонд функционально взаимосвязанных учреждений]

S —

GENERAL RECORDS SCHEDULE

A *records schedule* governing specified *series* of *records (1)* common to several or all agencies. Sometimes called common records schedule or general schedule (US).

D —

G Aussonderungs- und Bewertungs-Richtlinien für Fachneutrales Schriftgut

I Massimario generale di conservazione e/o di scarto, titolario

[Règlement de tri]   213

Règlement s'appliquant au *tri* de *séries d'archives (1)* déterminées, communes à tous les bureaux.

R Перечень типовых документов, образующихся в деятельности министерств, ведомств и других учреждений и организаций с указанием сроков хранения документов.

S —

GENERAL SCHEDULE *See* GENERAL RECORDS SCHEDULE

GENERAL STATE ARCHIVES *See* CENTRAL ARCHIVES

GENERATION

The degree of remoteness of a *copy*, usually photographic, from the *original*.

D Generatie

G Generation

I Tradizione

[Génération]   214

Place d'une *copie* dans l'ensemble des *reproductions*, généralement photographiques, dérivant successivement les unes des autres à partir de l'*original*.

R [Степень адэкватности, соответствия копии оригиналу]

S Generación

GEOGRAPHICAL ARRANGEMENT *See* ARRANGEMENT

GIFT

An addition to *holdings* acquired without monetary consideration and becoming the sole property of

DON   215

Entrée de *documents (1)* dans un *dépôt* d'*archives (2)* résultant d'une cession de propriété par une personne

the recipient, frequently effected by a *deed* or *instrument* of gift.

D Schenking

G Schenkung, Geschenk

I Dono

privée, physique ou morale, faite à titre gratuit et souvent confirmée par un *acte* écrit et irrévocable.

R Дарение документов

S Donación, donativo

GUARD

A strip of *paper* or cloth attached to or replacing the binding edge of a *leaf* or *sheet*. *See also* TIPPING-IN.

D [Verbindingsstrook]

G Falzstreifen

I Brachetta

ONGLET   216

(1) En *reliure*: étroite bande de *papier* insérée à une place déterminée parmi les *cahiers* d'un *volume* lors de sa *reliure* pour y coller un *feuillet (1)* supplémentaire.

(2) En *restauration*: étroite bande de *papier* réunissant à nouveau par collage les deux bords déchirés d'un *feuillet*.

R [Укрепление краев документа при переплете]

S Cartivana, escartivana

GUIDE

(1) A *finding aid,* giving a general account of all or part of the *holdings* of one or several *archives (3)* including the administrative or other background history, usually arranged by *record/archive group* or *fonds* and *classes* or *series* therein. *See also* SUMMARY OF RECORDS.

(2) A *finding aid* describing the *holdings* of one or more *archives (3)* relating to particular subjects, periods, or geographical areas or to specified types or categories of *documents*.

D (1) Overzicht van archieven
   (2) Archiefgids

G (1) Beständeübersicht, (Archiv)-
      Führer

(1) GUIDE PAR DÉPÔTS   217

Instrument de recherche fournissant une vue générale de l'ensemble des *fonds* et *collections* d'un ou de plusieurs services d'*archives (2)*, généralement présentés par *fonds* ou par *séries*, dont chacun est complété par un historique de l'administration productrice et par la liste des *instruments de recherche* correspondants.

(2) GUIDE SPÉCIALISÉ

Instrument de recherche décrivant les *fonds* et *collections* d'un ou de plusieurs services d'*archives (2)* relatives à des thèmes, à des périodes, à des espaces géographiques, à des types de *documents* particuliers, prédéfinis.

R (1) Путеводитель по архиву (архивам)
   (2) Тематический путеводитель по архиву (архивам)

(continued)

(2) Sachthematischer Führer, -s
Inventar

I (1) Guida generale
(2) Guida tematica

S (1/2) Guía

HAND LAMINATION

A manual process for protecting
or reinforcing a weak or damaged
paper document by enclosing it
between two sheets of cellulose
acetate, with thin tissue, which
are bound to the *document* by
acetone. Also called solvent
lamination. *See also* THERMO-
PLASTIC LAMINATION.

D Lamineren, doubleren

G Einbettung, Handlaminierung

I Laminazione a freddo

LAMINATION MANUELLE 218

Procédé de *restauration,* parfois de
simple protection, d'un *document (1)*
détérioré sur *papier*, généralement après
désacidification, par compression à la
main de celui-ci entre deux *feuilles*
d'acétate de cellulose, parfois renforcées
de tissu mince, et collées grâce à une
application d'acétone. *Voir* (475)
LAMINATION THERMOPLASTIQUE.

R Ламинирование ручным
способом

S Laminación manual

HARD COPY

A *document* or *copy,* usually on
paper, as opposed to a *microform*
or *machine-readable record.*

D Hard copy

G Aufsichtskopie, Papierkopie

I Copia su carta

DOCUMENT EN CLAIR 219

Document ou *reproduction* de *document* généralement sur *papier*, par opposition à *copie* sur *microforme* ou à
document lisible par machine.

R [Документ на бумажной
основе]

S Copia en papel

HARDWARE

The physical units making up a
computer system as distinct
from *software.*

D Apparatuur, hardware

G Hardware

I Hardware, componenti materiali
di elaboratore

MATÉRIEL 220

Eléments physiques constitutifs d'un
ordinateur, de ses satellites ou de
ses auxiliaires; s'oppose à *logiciel*.

R Аппаратные средства в вычислительной машине

S Material o equipo informativo

HERALDRY

The science dealing with
armorial bearings.

HÉRALDIQUE 221

Science des armoiries.

D Heraldiek, wapenkunde

G Wappenkunde, Heraldik

I Araldica

R Геральдика

S Heráldica

HISTORICAL ARCHIVES

Archives (2) which do not receive further regular *accessions* or *accruals. See also* CLOSED RECORD GROUP.

D —

G Historische(s) Archiv(e)

I Archivio storico, archivio morto

ARCHIVES HISTORIQUES 222

Archives (2) ne recevant plus de *versements* réguliers. *Voir aussi* (91) SÉRIE CLOSE.

R Исторический архив

S Archivo histórico

HISTORICAL EDITING

The processes involved in the preparation of a *documentary publication.*

D [Verzorgen van bronnenpublik-aties]

G (Historische) Editionstätig-keit, -technik

I Edizioni di documenti

[Edition historique] 223

Ensemble des recherches scientifiques qu'implique la préparation de *publications de documents.*

R Публикационная деятель-ность. Археографическая деятель-ность

S Edición de documentos

HISTORICAL MANUSCRIPTS *See* MANUSCRIPTS

HOLDINGS

The totality of *records (1)/ archives (1)* in the *custody* of a *records centre/archives (2).*Also referred to as *collections.*

D Bestand

G Gesamtbestand (eines Archivs (2))

I Insieme dei fondi

FONDS ET COLLECTIONS 224

Ensemble des *documents* conservés dans un service d'*archives (2).*

R Комплекс фондов архива, Состав фондов архива

S Fondos

HOLOGRAPH

A *document* entirely in the handwriting of the person who signed it.

OLOGRAPHE 225

Document entièrement écrit à la main du signataire; se dit plus spécialement d'un testament.

(continued)

D Holograaf

G Eigenhändiges Schreiben,
Autograph

I Olografo, autografo

R Автограф

S Ológrafo

HONEYCOMBING
The process of deliberately
leaving space in *stack areas* for
future *accessions* or *accruals* to
*record/archive groups, sub-groups,
classes* or *series* already accessioned
in part.

D –

G Lagerung 'auf Lücke'

I –

RANGEMENT DISCONTINU   226
Procédé de rangement *d'archives*
réservant des espaces libres entre
les *fonds,* les *séries* et les *sous-
séries* pour y insérer leurs
accroissements successifs.

R [Оставление свободных
мест на стеллажах для
новых поступлений]

S Colocación espaciada

HORIZONTAL FILING *See* FLAT FILING

HOUSEKEEPING RECORDS
Records (1) that relate to budget,
personnel, supply, and similar
facilitative operations as distinct
from substantive or *programme
records* (US).

D [Archiefbescheiden betreffende
het organisme]

G Fachneutrales Schriftgut;
Schriftgut der Dienststellen-
verwaltung

I –

[– – –]   227
Documents produits par les seules
activités de fonctionnement interne:
budget, équipement, bâtiment, per-
sonnel(U.S.).

R Административно-хозяй-
ственные документы

S Documentos de gestión

HUMIDIFICATION
(1) The placing of dry and brittle
documents in moisture-laden
air, in a cloud chamber or
container to aid in the gradual
absorption of water vapour for
added pliability. *See also*
FLATTENING.
(2) The increase of the moisture
content in an archival storage
area.

HUMIDIFICATION   228
(1) Procédé de *conservation (2)
d'archives (1)* consistant à placer
dans une atmosphère humide des
documents desséchés ou cassants,
afin de leur restituer leur souplesse
par absorption graduelle de vapeur
d'eau.
(2) Accroissement du degré
hydrométrique dans les locaux de
conservation *d'archives (1).*

(continued)

D (1) Bevochtiging
  (2) Luchtbevochtiging

G (1) Befeuchtung
  (2) Luftbefeuchtung

I (1) Umidificazione
  (2) Aumento dell' umidità
     relativa

R (1/2) Увлажнение документов, воздуха

S (1/2) Humidificación

HYGROMETER
An instrument for measuring
relative humidity.

D Hygrometer

G Hygrometer, Feuchtigkeits-
  messer

I Igrometro

HYGROMÈTRE 229
Appareil fixe ou mobile destiné
à mesurer le degré d'humidité
relative de l'air dans un local clos.

R Гигрометр

S Higrómetro

ICONOGRAPHIC RECORDS/ARCHIVES
Documents in the form of pictures,
photographs, illustrations, *prints
(2)* and the products of other
pictorial processes with related
textual records/archives. See also
PHOTOGRAPHIC RECORDS/
ARCHIVES.

D [Inconografische archiefbeschei-
  den]

G Bilddokumente, -archiv(e)

I Documenti iconografici,
  archivio iconografico

ARCHIVES ICONOGRAPHIQUES 230
Ensemble de *documents* se présentant sous forme d'*images* manuscrites,
imprimées, photographiques ou
autres, et de textes s'y rapportant.
Voir (363) ARCHIVES PHOTO-
GRAPHIQUES.

R Изобразительные документы

S Documentos/archivos
  iconográficos

IMAGE
A *reproduction* of the subject
matter copied, usually by
photography.

D Afbeelding

G Bild, Abbildung

I Immagine

IMAGE 231
Reproduction d'un objet, la copie
étant habituellement réalisée par
photographie.

R Изображение

S Imagen

IMPRESCRIPTIBILITY

The concept that *archives (2)* which are inalienable remain subject to *replevin* without limitation of time. *See also* INALIENABILITY.

D Onverjaarbaarheid

G Unverjährbarkeit (des Anspruchs auf Herausgabe entfremdeten öffentlichen Archivguts)

I Imprescrittibilità

IMPRESCRIPTIBILITÉ 232

Concept selon lequel les *archives (1)* publiques, qui sont inaliénables, peuvent être revendiquées sans limitation dans le temps.

R —

S Imprescriptibilidad

INACTIVE RECORDS *See* NON-CURRENT RECORDS

INALIENABILITY

The quality of *archives (1)* deriving from their relationship to the sovereignty of a state or the legal authority of any other body, which prevents their removal or abandonment or the transfer of ownership contrary to law. Also called inviolability. *See also* IMPRESCRIPTIBILITY.

D Onvervreembaarheid

G Unveräußerlichkeit

I Inalienabilità

INALIÉNABILITÉ 233

Caractère que présentent les *archives (1)* publiques du fait de leur domanialité et qui interdit leur cession à des tiers. *Voir* (232) IMPRESCRIPTIBILITÉ.

R [Неотчуждаемость докумен-тов архива]

S Inalienabilidad

INCINERATION

The *destruction* of *documents* by burning.

D Verbranding, verassing

G (Akten)Verbrennung

I Incenerimento

INCINÉRATION 234

Destruction volontaire de *documents* par le feu.

R Сжигание

S Incineración

INDEFINITE VALUE *See* ARCHIVAL VALUE

INDENTURE *See* CHIROGRAPH

INDEX

A *list* of persons, places and/or subjects referred to in a

INDEX 235

Liste alphabétique des noms de personnes, des noms géographiques

(continued)

document or finding aid with location of references thereto, usually in alphabetical order.

D Index

G Index

I Indice, repertorio

et des noms de matières contenus dans un *document d'archives (1)* assortie des références correspondantes destinées à les localiser. *Voir aussi* (476) THESAURUS.

R Указатель

S Indice

INDEX OF USERS/USES

An *index* of persons, agencies, institutions or organisations who have requested *documents* or *information* from *documents,* and/or of the subject matter on which *information* has been requested.

D Bezoekersregister

G Benutzerkartei

I Schedario degli studiosi, degli argomenti di ricerca e dei fondi consultati

(1) FICHIER DES LECTEURS   236
Fichier alphabétique des personnes, des administrations, des organismes qui ont demandé la consultation de *documents* ou des informations contenues dans les *documents.*
(2) FICHIER DES RECHERCHES
Fichier alphabétique et/ou méthodique des thèmes de recherches opérées dans un service d'*archives (2).*

R [картотеки: социально-
   биографических, темати-
   ческих запросов, исследователей читальных
   залов]

S Indice/lista de consultantes, lista de consultas

INFORMATION

Recorded *data (1)*.

D Informatie

G Information

I Informazioni, notizie

DONNÉES ENREGISTRÉES /   237
DONNÉES INFORMATISÉES
Données (1) mises en *mémoire (2)* dans un *ordinateur.*

R Информация.
  документная информация

S Información

INFORMATION MANAGEMENT

The administration of *information,* its use and transmission, and the application of theories and techniques of *information science* to create, modify, or improve information handling systems.

GESTION DE L'INFORMATION   238
Gestion spécialisée dans l'information, son utilisation et sa circulation, et application de la théorie et des techniques de l'information à cette gestion.

D Informatiebeheer

G Informations-Organisation

I Gestione delle informazioni

R [управление информацион-
ной деятельностью
архивов]

S Tratamiento de la información

INFORMATION RETRIEVAL (SYSTEM)

A set of procedures, usually automated, by which references to or the *data (1)* contained in *documents* are indexed and stored in such a manner that they can be retrieved in response to specific requests.

D [Systeem voor het terugvinden van informatie]

G Informations-Retrieval (-System)

I Recupero automatico delle informazioni

RECHERCHE DOCUMENTAIRE 239

Ensemble des procédés, générale-ment automatiques, par lesquels des *données (1)* contenues dans des *documents* concernant un sujet donné peuvent être indexés, mises en réserve et extraites pour l'utilisateur.

R Автоматизированная информационно-поисковая
система

S Recuperación de la información

INFORMATION SCIENCE

The study of the theory and practice of the acquisition, processing and dissemination of *information.*

D Informatica

G Informatik, Informations-wissenschaft

I Informatica

SCIENCE DE L'INFORMATION 240

Discipline traitant de la théorie et de la pratique de la collecte, du *traitement* et de la diffusion de l'information.

R Информатика

S Ciencia de la información

INFORMATIONAL VALUE

The value of *records (1)/ archives (1)* for reference and research deriving from the *in-formation* they contain as distinct from their *evidential value.*

D [Informatiewaarde]

G Nachrichtlicher Wert

I Valore informativo

[– – –] 241

Valeur d'information des *documents* utilisés à des fins de référence ou de recherche, indépendamment de leur valeur de témoignage sur l'histoire de l'institution productrice; s'oppose à 'evidential value'.

R Информационная ценность
документа

S Valor informativo

INLAYING *See* FRAMING

IN-LETTER
Correspondence received by an
agency, institution or organisation and sometimes maintained in
a separate *series. See also*
OUT-LETTER.

D Ingekomen stukken

G Eingang, Einlauf

I Lettera ricevuta

CORRESPONDANCE PASSIVE 242
Toute espèce de communication
écrite reçue par une institution ou
un organisme, parfois conservée dans
une *série* indépendante; dite aussi
correspondance reçue ou arrivée.

R Входящий документ

S Correspondencia

INPUT-OUTPUT
(1) The equipment used to
communicate with a *computer.*
(2) The *data (1)* involved in such
communication.
(3) The *medium* carrying the
data (1) involved in such communication.

D Invoer-uitvoer, input-output

G (1) Dateneingabe, -ausgabe
(2) Eingabe-, Ausgabedaten
(3) Datenträger (für Ein- und
Ausgabe)

I (1/2/3) Entrata-uscita

ENTRÉE – SORTIE 243
(1) Equipement utilisé pour communiquer avec un *ordinateur.*
(2) *Données (1)* utilisées dans ce type
de communication.
(3) *Support* des *données (1)* utilisées
dans ce type de communication.

R (1) Ввод-вывод, устройство
ввода-вывода информации

S (1/2/3) Entrada-salida

INSPECTION, RIGHT OF
The legally imposed responsibility
of *archives (2)* or a *records
management* service to inspect
and report, and to propose
measures to improve the records
creation, maintenance, and
disposal practices of operating
agencies within its jurisdiction.

D Inspectiebevoegdheid

G Inspektionsrecht

I Sorveglianza (sugli uffici
statali), vigilanza (sugli
enti pubblici non statali e
privati)

DROIT D'INSPECTION 244
Fonction réglementaire, dévolue à
un service d'*archives (2),* de contrôler
la création, la *conservation* et le
rangement des *documents* par des
administrations soumises à sa juridiction et de prescrire les mesures
adéquates.

R Инспектирование, контроль
за организацией докумен-
тов в делопроизводстве

S Derecho de inspección

INSPEXIMUS *See* VIDIMUS

INSTRUMENT
A formal legal *document*, such
as a *deed* or contract.

D Instrument

G (Notariats-) Instrument;
(*sonst.*) Urkunde

I Instrumento, istromento
(soltanto notarile); documento,
contratto, apoca (senza
intervento del notaio)

INSTRUMENT   245
Document authentique établissant
un droit privé ou public.

R [Официальный документ,
имеющий юридическую силу]

S Instrumento

INTELLECTUAL PROPERTY *See* COPYRIGHT

INTERMEDIATE REPOSITORY *See* RECORDS CENTRE

INTERMEDIATE STORAGE
The storage of *semi-current
records* in a *records centre*
pending their ultimate
disposal.

D [Plaatsing in een tussen-
archief]

G Zwischenlagerung

I Prearchiviazione

PRÉARCHIVAGE   246
Gestion des *archives (1)* entre leur
sortie des bureaux producteurs et
leur entrée dans un service d'*archives (2)*, impliquant leur *conservation*
dans un local spécifique dit *centre
de préarchivage* ou *dépôt* intermédiaire
et la préparation de leur *versement*,
éventuellement après *tri.*

R [Промежуточный архив]

S Depósito intermedio

INTRINSIC VALUE
The inherent value of a *document*
dependent upon some unique
factor, such as content, usage,
circumstances surrounding its
creation, *signature (1)*, attached
seal(s) (2).

D [Intrinsieke waarde]

G Äußerer (nicht inhaltsbezogener
Wert)

I Valore intrinseco

VALEUR INTRINSÈQUE   247
Valeur propre d'un *document*
dépendant des facteurs tels que
son contenu, les circonstances de
sa production, la présence ou non
de *signature(s) (1)*, de *sceau(x) (2).*

R [Ценность документа по его
происхождению, назначению,
содержанию, удостоверению]

S Valor intrínseco

INVENTORY

(1) A *finding aid* listing and describing in varying degrees of detail the contents of one or more *record/archive groups, fonds, classes* or *series*, usually including a brief history of the organisation and functions of the originating agency/ies, institutions or organisations and, if appropriate, *indexes.* In US usage, the normal unit of *entry (3)* is the *series.* According to the degree of descriptive detail, an *inventory (1)* may be referred to an an analytical inventory *(calendar)*, descriptive inventory or *list,* preliminary inventory, repertory or summary inventory.

(2) A *document* containing a *list* of things, e.g. furniture and fittings, often, as in the case of the property of deceased persons, with an indication of value.

D (1) Inventaris
  (2) Inventaris, boedelbeschrijving

G (1) Inventar, Repertorium
  (2) Inventar

I (1/2) Inventario

INVENTAIRE 248

(1) *Instrument de recherche* fournissant une énumération descriptive plus ou moins détaillée des *dossiers* ou des *pièces* composant un ou plusieurs *fonds d'archives* ou *séries*, le plus souvent complété par un historique de l'institution productrice et de ses *archives (1)*, par l'exposé des principes de *classement* apportés et par un *index.* Selon le détail des renseignements fournis, un *inventaire (1)* peut être analytique *(registre, catalogue)*, descriptif *(répertoire)*, par échantillon *(inventaire sommaire)*, chronologique (regeste chronologique), ou provisoire.

(2) *Document* contenant une énumération parfois descriptive d'objets, établi pour des besoins divers, ainsi après un décès, après une saisie, ou en vue d'un partage.

R (1) Архивная опись
  (2) Инвентаризационная опись

S (1/2) Inventario

INVENTORY ROOM

A room in *archives (3)* in which *finding aids* are available for consultation by *users;* also referred to as catalogue room. *See also* SEARCH ROOM.

D [Inventarissenkamer]

G Repertorienzimmer, Findbuchzimmer

I Sala degli inventari

SALLE DES INVENTAIRES 249

Salle spécialisée d'un service d'*archives (2)* où des *instruments de recherche* de toute nature sont offerts à la consultation des *lecteurs.*

R [Отдел информационно-поисковых систем архива]

S Sala de inventarios

INVIOLABILITY *See* INALIENABILITY

ITEM
The basic unit of *arrangement* and *description*, normally bearing its own unique *reference number:* in UK also called *piece.*

D Nummer

G (Verzeichnungs)Einheit

I Unità archivistica, pezzo archivistico

(1) ARTICLE 250
Unité de base, pour la *cotation,* le rangement et l'*inventaire* des *documents d'archives;* l'article est généralement un *carton,* une *liasse,* un *volume* ou un *rouleau.*
(2) PIÈCE
La plus petite unité archivistique indivisible; elle peut être constituée d'un ou plusieurs *feuillets,* d'un *cahier* ou d'un *volume.*

R (1) Единица хранения архивных документов
(2) архивный документ

S Unidad documental, pieza

JOINT ARCHIVES /
JOINT HERITAGE
Archives (1) forming part of the national heritage of two or more states, which cannot be physically divided without destroying their *archival integrity.*

D —

G Gemeinschaftliches Archiv, Samtarchiv

I Archivi communi a due stati

[Patrimoine archivistique commun] 251
Archives (1) formant une part du patrimoine national d'un ou de plusieurs états, qui ne peuvent être divisées sous peine de perdre leur valeur administrative, légale ou historique.

R [Единое документальное наследие двух и более государств]

S Archivos conjuntos

JOURNAL
A daily *record* of events, financial transactions or the proceedings of a legislative or other body.

D Dagboek

G Journal, Tagebuch

I Libro giornale (di contabilità), diario, registro dei verbali (de un'assemblea)

JOURNAL (2) 252
Enregistrement au jour de jour d'événements, de réflexions, d'opérations financières ou de *procès-verbaux* d'une personne physique ou morale.

R Журнал
S Diario

KEYWORD
A word or group of words taken from the title or text of a *document* characterising its

NOM DE MATIÈRE 253
Mot ou groupe de mots emprunté au titre ou au texte d'un *document* pour en caractériser le contenu et en

(continued)

content and facilitating its
retrieval. *See also*
THESAURUS.

faciliter le repérage, spécialement
employé dans les *index;* dit aussi mot-
clé ou vedette-matière. *Voir aussi* (476)
THESAURUS.

D Trefwoord, lemma

G Stichwort

I Parola chiave

R Ключевое слово

S Palabra clave

LABEL

(1) A piece of material affixed to
the front or spine of a *file (1)*,
volume, box or other container
upon which a *reference number*
or other *information* is recorded
to facilitate storage and
retrieval.
(2) In *automatic data processing*
a *code (1)* used to idetify an item
of *data (1)*, an area of *memory*,
a *record (2)* or a *file (3)*.

(1) ÉTIQUETTE   254

Morceau de *papier* ou de *carton*
fixé sur le plat ou sur la tranche
d'un *article (liasse, registre, carton)*
et porteur d'une *cote*, d'un groupe
de *cotes* ou de toute autre information
permettant de le ranger ou de le
retrouver.
(2) LABEL
En *traitement automatique des
données* (1), enregistrement spécial
servant à identifier une *donnée* (1),
une partie de *mémoire (2)*, un
enregistrement ou un *fichier*.

D (1) Etiket
   (2) Etiket, label

G (1) Etikett
   (2) Label

I (1) Etichetta, targhetta
   (2) Etichetta

R (1) Ярлык, этикетка
   (2) Метка

S (1) Tejuelo
   (2) Etiqueta

LABELLING

In the course of *arrangement (2)*,
the process of preparing and
affixing *labels*.

D Etiketteren

G Etikettieren

I Etichettatura, targhettatura

ÉTIQUETAGE   255

Préparation et fixation d'*étiquettes*.

R Написание и приклеивание
  ярлыков, этикетов

S Entejuelar

LAMINATION *See* HAND LAMINATION: THERMOPLASTIC LAMINATION

LANTERN SLIDE

A photographic *slide* for projection, originally, by magic
lantern.

D Lantaarnplaatje, dia

G Glasbild, Diapositiv

I Diapositiva

DIAPOSITIVE 256

Image positive sur *support*
transparent destinée à la projection.

R Слайд

S Diapositiva

LEAF

A *sheet* of *paper* or *parchment*
each side of which is referred to
as a *page*.

D Blad

G Blatt

I Carta, foglio

FEUILLET (2) 257

Ensemble formé par le recto et le
verso — appelés pages — d'une
feuille de papier ou de *parchemin*.

R [Лист, нумеруемый с обеих
сторон]

S Hoja, folio

LEDGER

The *volume* of final entry in
accounting in which are entered
debits, credits, and all other
money transactions under each
individual account or heading.

D Grootboek

G Hauptbuch

I Libro mastro

GRAND LIVRE 258

Registre financier où sont inscrits
des *comptes* définitifs et où les débits
et les crédits, ainsi que toutes autres
opérations comptables, sont ventilés par
chapitres et par articles.

R Главная книга

S Libro mayor

LEGAL CUSTODY *See* CUSTODY

LEGAL DEPOSIT

The legal requirement that free
copies of all works printed or
published in a country be placed
in specified *respositories* in that
country.

D Wettelijk depot

G Abgabepflicht (für Bücher und
Drucksachen)

I Deposito legale (bibl.)

DÉPÔT LÉGAL 259

Remise obligatoire et gratuite à un
service d'*archives* (2) publiques ou
à une bibliothèque publique, d'un
ou de plusieurs exemplaires de toute
publication imprimée dans le pays,
conformément aux dispositions
légales.

R Депонирование опублико-
ванных работ, печатных
изданий

S Depósito legal

LEGAL VALUE

The value of *records (1)/archives (1)* for the conduct of current or future legal business and/or as evidence thereof. *See also* ADMINISTRATIVE VALUE: FISCAL VALUE.

D Bewijswaarde, bewijskracht

G Rechtlicher (Beweis)wert

I Valore legale

VALEUR LÉGALE 260

(1) [Valeur que représente un *document,* pour l'administration d'origine ou son successeur, dans la conduite des affaires nécessitant le recours en droit.]
(2) Valeur inhérente à certaines catégories de *documents* permettant la défense des droits des personnes physiques ou morales. *Voir aussi* (170) VALEUR PROBATOIRE.

R (1) Юридическая ценность документа
(2) [Практическая ценность документов для администрации]

S Valor legal

LETTER

(1) A written message, now usually sent by mail in an *envelope.*
(2) An official *document* conferring specified powers or privileges. *See also* LETTER(S) CLOSE: LETTER(S) PATENT.

D (1) Brief
(2) Akte

G (1) Brief, Schreiben
(2) Brief

I (1) Lettera
(2) Diploma, privilegio, patente

LETTRE 261

(1) Communication écrite adressée à une personne publique ou privée et, de nos jours, généralement envoyée sous *enveloppe* par voie postale.
(2) *Document* officiel conférant des pouvoirs ou accordant des privilèges déterminés. *Voir aussi* (263) LETTRE CLOSE, (264) LETTRE PATENTE.

R (1) Писмо. Грамота
(2) [Официальный документ, содержащий какие-либо полномочия]

S (1) Carta
(2) Privilegio

LETTERBOOK

A *volume* in which *draft* or *fair copy letters (1)* sent have been written, usually in chronological order; also used for *copies* on single *sheets* of *letters (1)* sent, subsequently bound together. *See also* LETTERPRESS COPYBOOK.

REGISTRE D'ENREGISTREMENT DU COURRIER 262

Registre dans lequel sont transcrits, généralement dans un ordre chronologique, les *lettres (1)* au départ ou /et à l'arrivée, ou leur analyse plus ou moins détaillée. *Voir aussi* (265) REGISTRE DE COPIES LITHOGRAPHIQUES.

D Brievenboek

G Briefbuch

I Registro delle copie delle
lettere spedite, copialettere

R Дело, содержащее пере-
писку, подшивка писем

S Libro copiador de cartas

LETTER(S) CLOSE

A *letter (2)* , to a specified
addressee and closed with a
seal (2) to keep its contents
private. UK usage is normally
plural.

D Besloten brief

G Geschlossener Brief

I Lettera chiusa, dispaccio
sigillato

LETTRE CLOSE 263

Lettre (2) de chancellerie adressée à
une seule personne et close par un
sceau (2) pour en conserver secret
le contenu.

R —

S Carta cerrada

LETTER(S) PATENT

A formal open *letter (2)* issued
under a *seal (2)* in favour of a
specified addressee but addressed
generally, so as to make known
the contents. UK usage is normally
plural.

D Open brief

G Offener Brief, Patent

I Lettere patenti, patente

LETTRES PATENTES 264

Acte de chancellerie en forme de
lettre (2) solennelle scellée exprimant
et rendant publique la volonté d'une
autorité souveraine.

R Жалованная грамота,
патент

S Carta patente, letra(s)
patente(s)

LETTERPRESS COPYBOOK

A *letterbook* of tissue *paper* in
which *copies* are recorded by
transfer of ink through direct
contact with the *original*, using
moisture and pressure in a copy
press. A single *copy* produced
by this method is referred to as
a letterpress copy or press copy.

D Kopieboek

G Briefkopierbuch

I Registro copialettere

REGISTRE DE COPIES 265
LITHOGRAPHIQUES

Type de *registre* de correspondance
dans lequel sont enregistrées des
copies établies par contact direct
avec l'*original* grâce à un transfert
d'encre par pression humide; la
copie produite est dite *copie
lithographique*.

R [Подшивка печатных копий]

S [Libro copiador de cartas]

LINEAR FEET/METRES

A measurement, for descriptive and control purposes, of *shelf* space occupied by *records (1)/archives (1)* and of the length of each unit of *film, tape,* or *microfilm.*

D Strekkende meter

G Laufende Meter, Regalmeter

I Piede/metri lineare

MÈTRE LINÉAIRE 266

Unité conventionnelle de mesure utilisée à des fins de contrôle ou de description et servant à évaluer soit la longueur occupée ou à occuper sur les *rayonnages* par des *documents,* soit la longueur d'une unité de *film,* de *bande magnétique* ou de *microfilm.*

R Погонный метр

S Metros lineales

LIST

An enumeration of *records (1)/archives (1)* at the level of *record/archive groups, fonds, classes, series, items* or *documents* and also of *holdings, accessions, finding aids,* etc. compiled for purposes of control and/or information. *See also* CHECKLIST.

D Lijst

G Liste

I Inventario, guida, elenco

(1) LISTE 267

Énumération d'*archives (1)* au niveau des *fonds,* des sous-fonds, des *séries,* des *articles* ou des *pièces,* ainsi que des *entrées* et des *instruments de recherche,* établie à des fins de contrôle ou d'information.

(2) BORDEREAU

Énumération de *pièces* ou d'*articles,* établie à l'occasion d'un *versement* ('bordereau de versement'), d'une opération d'*élimination* ('bordereau d'élimination'), d'un transfert quelconque ('bordereau d'envoi') ou simplement pour décrire les *pièces* contenues dans un *dossier (1).*

R Перечень, список

S Inventario

LITERARY ARCHIVES

(1) *Archives (1)* of individual authors, literary organisations and/or institutions.
(2) *Archives (2)* responsible for the *acquisition, preservation* and *communication* of such *archives (1).*

ARCHIVES LITTÉRAIRES 268

(1) *Archives (1)* résultant des activités de personnalités, institutions ou sociétés littéraires.
(2) Services d'*archives (2)* chargé de la collecte, de la *conservation* et de la *communication* de ces *archives (1).*

(continued)

D (1/2) Letterkundige archieven

G (1/2) Literaturarchiv(e)

I (1) Archivi della letteratura
   (2) Archivio di litterati

R (1) Архивный фонд деятелей или учреждений ли-
тературы

S (1/2) Archivo literario

LITERARY MANUSCRIPTS
Manuscripts, including *drafts* and proofs, of literary texts.

D Literaire manuscripten

G Literarische Manuskripte, -Handschriften

I Manoscritti

MANUSCRITS LITTÉRAIRES 269
Travaux littéraires aux divers stades de leur élaboration: *brouillons*, textes définitifs, *épreuves.*

R Литературные рукописи

S Manuscritos literarios

LITERARY PROPERTY RIGHT *See* COPYRIGHT

LOAN
The temporary physical *transfer* of *archives (1)* to an outside location for reference or consult-ation, *reproduction,* research or *exhibition* purposes.

D Uitlening

G Ausleihe

I Prestito

COMMUNICATION AVEC 270
DÉPLACEMENT
Transfert temporaire, à l'extérieur, de *documents* appartenant à un service *d'archives (2)* à des fins de recherche, d'*exposition* ou de *reproduction.*

R Выдача документов во вре-
менное пользование учреж-
дениям

S Préstamo

LOCAL ARCHIVES
(1) *Archives (1)* of municipalities or other local government authorities.
(2) *Archives (2)* responsible for the *acquisiton, preservation* and *communication* of such *archives (1).*

D (1) Lokale, plaatselijke
     archieven
   (2) Lokale, plaatselijke
     archiefdienst

G (1/2) Kommunalarchive

I (1/2) Archivi di enti locali

ARCHIVES COMMUNALES 271
(1) Ensemble des *archives (1)* reçues et produites par l'administration d'une commune.
(2) Service d'*archives (2)* chargé de la collecte, de la *conservation* et de la *communication* de ces *archives (1).*

R (1) Архивные фонды местных
     учреждений
   (2) Местные архивы

S (1/2) Archivo(s) municipal(es)

LOCATION INDEX/REGISTER

A *finding aid* to control and locate
holdings. See also SHELF LIST.

D Depotlijst

G Lagerungsübersicht, Lagerkonkordanz

I Guida topografica

REGISTRE TOPOGRAPHIQUE 272

Instrument de recherche indiquant,
à des fins de contrôle ou de localisation, la place occupée dans les
archives (2) par chaque *article*,
identifiée par la référence au *magasin*,
à la *travée* et à la *tablette. Voir* (438)
INVENTAIRE TOPOGRAPHIQUE.

R Топографический указатель

S Indice topográfico

MACERATION

The destruction of documents by
soaking them in liquid in order
to decompose them. Also called
pulping.

D Maceratie

G Einstampf(en)

I Macero

PILON CHIMIQUE 273

Procédé de destruction de *documents*
par bain dans un liquide décomposant
le *papier.*

R [уничтожение документов
путем размачивания]

S Maceración

MACHINE READABLE RECORDS/ ARCHIVES

Records (1)/archives (1) usually
in *code (2)*, recorded on a *medium*
such as a *magnetic disc, magnetic
tape, punched card*, whose contents
are accessible only by machine and
organised in accordance with the
principle of provenance as distinct
from *data archive(s).*

D Machine-leesbare archiefbescheiden

G Maschinenlesbare Dokumente,
-Archive

I Documenti/archivi automatizzati

ARCHIVES INFORMATIQUES 274

Ensemble d'*archives (1)* traditionnelles
et d'*archives* généralement codées,
lisibles uniquement par machines,
enregistrées sur des *supports* tels que
disques, tambours ou *bandes magnétiques, cartes* ou *bandes perforées*,
comprenant les *documents* prépa-
ratoires, les bordereaux de collecte,
les *documents* de traitement et les
produits de sortie obtenus par
l'informatique.

R Машиночитаемые документы

S Documentos legibles por
máquina

MAGNETIC DISC/DISK

A flat circular *medium* the surfaces
of which are covered with a magneti - ·

DISQUE MAGNÉTIQUE 275

Support circulaire plat dont les faces
sont recouvertes d'une couche

(continued)

zable layer permitting the recording
and storage of _data (1)_.

D Magneetschijf
G Magnetplatte
I Disco magnetico

magnétisable servant à l'enregistrement et à la conservation de
données (1).

R Магнитный диск
S Disco magnético

MAGNETIC TAPE
A tape coated with a magnetizable
material, capable of storing
information in the form of electro-
magnetic signals.

D Magneetband
G Magnetband
I Banda magnetica, nastro
   magnetico

BANDE MAGNÉTIQUE 276
Support formé par une _bande_ de
matière plastique souple revêtue sur
une face d'un enduit magnétisable
permettant d'enregistrer des informations sous forme de signes
électromagnétiques.

R магнитная лента
S Banda magnética

MAGNIFICATION
The linear ratio of the size of an
image to that of the _original
document_ when viewed through
or projected by an optical instrument. Also called enlargement
ratio.

D Vergrotingsfactor
G Vergrößerungsgrad
I Rapporto/fattore di
   ingradimento

ÉCHELLE D'AGRANDISSEMENT 277
Relations chiffrée existant entre
les dimensions d'un _document
original_ et les dimensions de son
image vu à travers ou projetée
par un instrument optique.

R [Увеличение изображения
   через оптическое
   устройство]
S Ampliación

MAIL MANAGEMENT
The application of _records
management_ principles and
techniques to the flow of mail
(US).

D Postbehandeling
G Organisation des Postlaufs
I Lavorazione della posta

[– – –] 278
Application au traitement du courrier
des principes et des techniques de la
gestion des _documents_ (US).

R [экспедиция учреждения]
S –

MANUSCRIPT
A handwritten or typed
document.

D. Manuscript

G Manuskript, Handschrift

I Documento scritto a mano
o a macchina

MANUSCRIPT COLLECTION
Collection (1), (2) and/or *(3)* of
manuscripts, usually having
historical or literary value or
significance; frequently used
to distinguish non-archival from
archival material. *See also*
PAPERS.

D Handschriftenverzameling,
handschriftencollectie

G Handschriftensammlung

I Collezione di manoscritti

MANUSCRIPT CURATOR
A person professionally occupied
in the administration of *manuscript collections.* In US,
manuscript curators frequently
use the title *archivist.*

D (Handschriften)conservator

G [Leiter einer Handschriftenabteilung in Bibliotheken]

I Conservatore di manoscritti

MANUSCRIPT DEPARTMENT/
REPOSITORY
An institution which collects
papers, manuscripts, and,

MANUSCRIT   279
Texte écrit à la main ou, par extension,
dactylographié. Aux USA, le terme
'manuscripts' correspond généralement
au terme français *'archives privées'.*

R Рукописный и машинописный
документ

S Manuscrito

COLLECTION DE MANUSCRITS/   280
FONDS DE MANUSCRITS
Ensemble de *manuscrits* d'origines
diverses, sans liens entre eux, réunis
par un particulier, une bibliothèque
ou un musée. Aux USA, le terme
'collection de manuscrits' correspond
généralement au terme français
'collection d'*archives privées'.*
Voir (338) PAPIERS (1).

R Коллекция рукописей

S Colección de manuscritos

[Conservateur de manuscrits]   281
Spécialiste chargé de l'*acquisition,*
de la *conservation* et de la
communication de *manuscrits;*
appelé, par extension, *archiviste* (US).

R Хранитель рукописей

S —

DÉPARTEMENT DES MANUSCRITS   282
Institution spécialisée, parfois section
d'une bibliothèque ou d'un musée,
chargée de la *conservation* des

frequently *records (1)/archives (1)* of other institutions, usually in accordance with a predetermined *acquisition* policy.

D Handschriftenafdeling

G Handschriftenabteilung

I Sezione manoscritti

manuscrits et / ou (aux USA) des *archives privées.*

R **Хранилище рукописей. Рукописные отделы библиотек и музеев**

S Sección de manuscritos

MANUSCRIPT GROUP

A body of *manuscripts,* comparable to a *record/archive* group. The term is most frequently used by *archives (2)* in dealing with *documents* received from non-official sources (US, Canada). *See also* PAPERS.

D Handschriftencollectie

G Handschriftenbestand, Nachlaß

I Fondo di manoscritti

[– – –]   28.

Voir (280) COLLECTION DE MANUSCRITS.

R **Архивная коллекция. Рукописное собрание**

S Fondo de manuscritos

MAP

A *document* depicting in graphic or photogrammetric form, normally to scale and usually on a flat *medium,* a selection of material or abstract features on or in relation to the surface of the earth or of a heavenly body. *See also* PLAN.

D Kaart

G (Land)Karte

I Mappa (a piccola scala), carta geografica (a grande scala)

CARTE   284

Document représentant sous forme graphique ou photogrammétrique, sur un *support* plat – pour les *cartes* modernes – à une échelle supérieure au 20.000^e, des caractéristiques physiques ou abstraites choisies, relatives à la surface de la terre ou à un corps céleste. *Voir aussi* (356) PLAN.

R **Карта**

S Mapa

MARGINALIA

Information recorded in the margin of a *document.* Also called marginal note(s).

APOSTILLE   285

Information portée en marge d'un *document,* dite aussi *note* ou *mention marginale.*

D Kanttekening

G Marginalien, Randvermerke

I Glosse, annotazioni marginali

R Заметки, пометы на полях
документа

S Nota marginal

MARKING *See* STAMPING

MASTER
A *copy* of a *document* or, in
some processes, the *original
document,* from which *copies*
can be made.

D Moederkopie

G Mutterkopie, Stammkopie

I Matrice

MATRICE   286
(1) *Document originale* servant
de base à la création de *copies.*
(2) *Matrice de sceau; voir* (427)

R[Оригинал документа при
копировании, матрица]

S Matriz

MASTER NEGATIVE
A *duplicate* of the camera *negative
film* used to generate *positive
prints (1).*

D [Moedernegatief]

G Originalnegativ

I Matrice negativa

NÉGATIF ORIGINAL   287
Double du *négatif* de caméra
destiné à produire des *épreuves*
positives.

R Дубль-негатив

S Negativo

MEANS OF REFERENCE *See* FINDING AID

MEDIUM
The physical material in or on
which *data (1)* may be recorded,
i.e. clay tablet, *papyrus, paper,
parchment, film, magnetic tape*
(plural: media).

D Drager

G Datenträger, Schriftträger,
Beschreibstoff

I Supporto

SUPPORT   288
Matériau de nature à recevoir des
informations écrites, sonores, électromagnétiques ou visuelles, tel que
papyrus, papier, métal, parchemin,
tissu, bois, *film, bande magnétique.*

R Носитель информации

S Soporte

MEMBRANE
A single skin of *parchment*.

D –

G Pergament(haut)

I Membrana (*antiq.*), pergamena

PEAU
Pièce de *parchemin*.

R [Мембрана]

S Pergamino

MEMORANDUM
(1) A *document* recording *inform-ation* used for internal communica-tion and intended for future referen-ce. *See also* NOTE.
(2) A *document* drawn up in support of a case in court or a request.

D (1) Memorandum, memo
(2) Memorie

G (1) Aktenvermerk, Denkschrift
(2) Prozess-Schrift

I (1) Promemoria, memorandum
(2) Comparsa, memoria di parte

(1) NOTE (1)
Document fournissant une informa-tion à usage interne et servant de référence ultérieure.
(2) MÉMOIRE (masc.) (1)
Document écrit destiné à soutenir une cause ou à étayer une requête.

R (1) Служебная записка
(2) Меморандум

S (1) Nota interior
(2) Memorial

MEMORANDUM BOOK *See* COMMONPLACE BOOK

MEMORY
In *automatic data processing,* any device into which *data (1)* can be recorded and stored and from which they can be retrieved.

D Geheugen

G (Daten)Speicher

I Memoria

MÉMOIRE (fém.) (2)
Dans le *traitement automatique des données,* tout organe permettant l'*enregistrement,* la *conservation* et la restitution de *données (1).*

R Память, запоминающее устройство

S Memoria

METRIC PAPER SIZE
An international system of *paper* measurement based on the sub-divisions of a square metre.

D Metriek papierformaat

G Metrische Papierformate

I Formato normalizzato della carta

FORMAT NORMALISÉ DU PAPIER
Définition internationale des dimen-sions du *papier* fondée sur les sub-divisions du mètre carré.

R [Нормативный формат бумаги]

S Formato normalizado de papel

METROLOGY
The science dealing with weights
and measures.

D Metrologie

G Maß- und Gewichtskunde,
Metrologie

I Metrologia

MÉTROLOGIE 293
Science appliquée à l'étude des
poids et mesures et à leurs rapports
au cours des temps.

R Метрология

S Metrología

MICROCARD
Microimages arranged in similar
manner to those on a *microfiche*
but on an opaque *medium*. Also
called micro-opaque: microprint.

D Microkaart

G Mikrokarte

I Microscheda (su supporto
opaco)

MICROCARTE 294
Micro-images juxtaposées
régulièrement sur un *support*
opaque.

R Микрокарта

S Microficha opaca

MICROCOMPUTER
A *computer* based on a *micro-
processor*, limited main *memory*
and backing storage on *magnetic
tape* in *cassettes* or on *floppy
discs/disks*, usually dedicated to
a single function. *See also*
MINICOMPUTER.

D Microcomputer

G Mikrocomputer

I Microelaboratore

MICRO-ORDINATEUR 295
Ordinateur de la forme la plus
simple, fondé sur l'utilisation d'un
microprocesseur et sur des *mémoires* (2)
externes, *disques souples, cassettes*
et petites imprimantes.
Voir aussi (306) MINI-ORDINATEUR.

R Микро-ЭВМ

S Microordenador

MICROCOPY
A *copy*, usually obtained by photography, in a size too small to be
read without magnification.

D Microkopie

G Mikrokopie

I Microcopia

MICROCOPIE 296
Réduction photographique d'un
document ne pouvant être lue
qu'avec un appareil agrandisseur.

R Микрофильм

S Microcopia

MICROFICHE
A flexible transparent sheet of
film bearing a number of *micro-*

MICROFICHE 297
Feuille de *film* transparent servant de
support à des *micro-images* disposées

109

(continued)

images arranged in horizontal rows and vertical columns, normally having an identifying strip legible without magnification.

D Microfiche

G Mikrofiche

I Microsheda (su supporto trasparente)

en quadrillage régulier, le plus souvent pourvue d'un titre directement lisible.

R Микрофиша

S Microficha

MICROFICHE CAMERA *See* STEP AND REPEAT CAMERA

MICROFILM

A fine-grain, high resolution *film* in *roll* form containing, after exposure, developing and fixing, an *image,* reduced in size from the *original.*

D Microfilm

G Mikrofilm

I Microfilm

MICROFILM 298

Rouleau de film transparent servant de *support* aux *images,* de format réduit et normalisé, d'un *original,* lisibles uniquement avec un appareil agrandisseur.

R Микрофильм

S Microfilme

MICROFILM CAMERA *See* PLANETARY CAMERA: ROTARY CAMERA

MICROFILM JACKET

A transparent holder into which individual strips of *microfilm* may be inserted.

D Microfilmjacket

G Mikrofilm-Jacket

I Jacket

JAQUETTE 299

Enveloppe transparente de format normalisé protégeant une *bande de microfilm* et généralement munie d'un titre lisible à l'oeil nu.

R Конверт для микрофильма в отрезке, джекет

S Funda

MICROFILM PUBLICATION

The publication on *microfilm,* usually in *roll* form, of *original documents* with necessary *targets* and explanatory materials.

PUBLICATION SUR MICROFILM 300

Edition sur *microfilm,* généralement en *rouleau (1)* de *documents d'archives* soit par *fonds* entiers ou parties de *fonds,* soit par sélection de *documents* relatifs à un thème donné, assortie de données explicatives, et destinée à la vente au public.

(continued)

D Microfilmpublikatie
G Mikrofilm-Publikation
I Microfilm

R Документальная публика-
    ция в виде микрофильма,
    сборник микрофильмов

S Publicación en microfilme

MICROFILM/MICROFICHE READER *See* READER/MICROFORM READER

MICROFILM STRIP
A segment of *roll microfilm*
that is usually inserted into a
microfilm jacket.

D Microfilmstrook
G Mikrofilmstreifen
I Striscia di microfilm,
  spezzone di pellicola

MICROFILM EN BANDE   301
Segment d'un *rouleau (1)* de
microfilm, composé de plusieurs
vues et généralement conservé sous
jaquette.

R Микрофильм в отрезке
S Tira de película

MICROFILM TARGET *See* TARGET

MICROFORM READER *See* READER

MICROFORMS
All *media* used to record *micro-
images.*

D Microvormen
G Mikroformen
I Microsupporti sensibili

MICROFORME   302
Terme générique désignant tout
type de *support* utilisé pour enregistrer
des *micro-images*, et chacun des
exemplaires réalisés.

R Пленка для микрофиль-
    мирования

S Microforma

MICROGRAPHICS
The technology and processes used
to record *information* on *micro-
forms.*
D Micrografie
G Mikrographie
I Micrografia

MICROGRAPHIE   303
Ensemble des procédés de *repro-
duction* de *documents* aboutissant
à une *microforme.*
R Микрофильмирование
S Micrografía

MICROIMAGE
An *image* too small to be read without *magnification*.

D Microbeeld
G Mikrobild
I Microimmagine

MICRO-IMAGE   304
Image de dimensions réduites ne pouvant être lue qu'avec un appareil agrandisseur.

R **Микроизображение**
S Microimagen

MICRO-OPAQUE *See* MICROCARD

MICROPHOTOGRAPHY *See* MICROGRAPHICS

MICROPRINT *See* MICROCARD

MICROPROCESSOR
A *central processing unit* contained on a single silicon chip.

D Microprocessor
G Mikroprocessor
I Microelaboratore

MICROPROCESSEUR   305
Unité centrale de traitement informatique contenu dans un seul circuit intégré, utilisable dans un *micro-ordinateur* ou tout autre dispositif automatique.

R **Микропроцессор**
S Microprocesador

MIGRATED ARCHIVES *See* REMOVED ARCHIVES

MINICOMPUTER
A general purpose *computer* of small size and able to operate in normal office environment.

D Minicomputer
G Minicomputer
I Minielaborate

MINI-ORDINATEUR   306
Type d'*ordinateur* simplifié, de volume et de coût réduits et ne nécessitant pas de conditions d'environnement particulières. *Voir aussi* (295) MICRO-ORDI-NATEUR.

R **Мини-ЭВМ**
S Miniordenador

MINISTERIAL ARCHIVES
Archives (1) or *archives (2)* of a

ARCHIVES MINISTÉRIELLES   307
Ensemble des *archives (1)* d'un

(continued)

ministry in the governmental structure.

D Ministeriearchief

G Ministerialakten, -archiv(e)

I Archivio ministeriale

ministère ou service d'*archives (2)* chargé de leur gestion.

R (1) Архивный фонд министерства
(2) Архив министерства

S Archivos ministeriales

MINUTE(S)

(1) A *note* or *memorandum*, specifically (plural), a *record (1)* of what was said and done at a meeting or conference.
(2) The final *draft* of a *document*.

D (1) Notulen
(2) Minuut

G (1) Protokoll, Aufzeichnung
(2) Reinkonzept

I (1) Verbale, processo verbale
(2) Minuta definitiva

(1) PROCÈS-VERBAL 308

Note (1) consignant les éléments essentiels ayant marqué le déroulement d'une réunion ou d'une conférence.
(2) MINUTE
Dernier brouillon d'un *document*.
(3) *Document* notarial possédant valeur d'*original*.

R (1) Протокол совещания
(2) Окончательный проект документа

S (1) Acta
(2) Minuta

MISSIVE *See* LETTER (1)

MOTION PICTURE(S)

A sequence of *photographs* on *roll film* or *videotape* which presents, as the *film* is advanced, the illusion of motion or movement. Also called moving images. Also called cinefilm (Canada), cinematograph film (Australia).

D Film

G Film, Spielfilm

I Film

FILM CINÉMATOGRAPHIQUE 309

Suite de prises de *vues* de petit format, juxtaposées en une seule série sur une pellicule, dont la projection produit l'illusion du mouvement.

R Кинодокумент, кинофильм

S Película

MOVING IMAGES *See* MOTION PICTURE(S)

MUNICIPAL ARCHIVES *See* LOCAL ARCHIVES

MUNIMENTS
Documents serving as evidence
of inheritance, title to property,
etc. (UK). *See also* CHARTER:
DEED.

D Titels

G Rechtstitel, Besitztitel

I Titoli giuridici

TITRE   310
Document consignant un *acte*
pouvant produire des effets
juridiques tels que l'héritage ou
la propriété. *Voir aussi* (126)
CONTRAT.

R [Документы подтверждающие
   права собственности,
   наследования и т.д.]

S Documentos probatorios

NATIONAL ARCHIVES
The *central archives* in a
national archival administration.

D [Nationaal archief]

G Nationalarchiv

I Archivio nazionale

ARCHIVES NATIONALES   311
Organisme chargé de la gestion des
archives (1) des institutions centrales d'une nation.

R (1) Центральный государ-
     ственный архив
   (2) [Национальный архив]

S Archivo nacional

NEGATIVE
A photographic *image* with
reversed *polarity* or, if coloured,
complementary tonal values to
those of the *original.*

D Negatief

G Negativ

I Negativo

NÉGATIF   312
Photographie originale ou *copie*
photographique présentant une
polarité inversée ou, si elles sont
colorées, des valeurs tonales
inversées.

R Негатив

S Negativo

NEGATIVE MICROFILM
A *microfilm* consisting of
negative images.

D. Negatieve microfilm

G Negativ(Mikro)film

I Microfilm negativo

MICROFILM NÉGATIF   313
Microfilm formé d'*images
négatives. Voir aussi* (312)
NÉGATIF.

R Негативный микрофильм

S Microfilme negativo

NON-CURRENT RECORDS
Records (1) no longer needed for
current business. *See also*
CURRENT RECORDS: SEMI-
CURRENT RECORDS.

[− − −]   314
Archives ayant perdu leur
utilité administrative courante.

(continued)

D Semistatische archief-
  bescheiden

G Altschriftgut, Altregistratur

I Archivio di deposito

R [Документы, утратившие
  практическое значение
  для учреждения]

S Documentos no vigente

NON-RECORD MATERIAL
Documentary materials not included
within the legal definition of
records (1) in some countries.

D [Niet-archiefmateriaal]

G Ergänzungsdokumentation

I Materiale non documentario

[− − −]   315
Matériau documentaire qui, dans
certains pays, n'est pas compris dans
la définition légale des *archives (1)*.

R −

S −

NOTARIAL ARCHIVES
Archives (1) arising from the
conduct of the business of
notaries public.

D Notariele archieven

G Notariatsakten, -archive

I Archivi notarili

ARCHIVES NOTARIALES   316
Archives (1) résultant des
activités des notaires.

R Архивные фонды нотариальных учреждений

S Archivo(s) notarial(es)

NOTE
(1) A brief statement of, e.g. a
fact or experience, written down
for review, or as an aid to
memory, or to inform someone
else. Also called a
memorandum.
(2) A short, informal *letter (1)*.
(3) A formal diplomatic or
    other official communica-
    tion.

D (1) Notitie, aantekening
  (2) Briefje, kattebelletje
  (3) Nota

G (1) (Akten)Vermerk,
      (Akten)Notiz
  (2) Notiz
  (3) Note

I (1) Nota, appunto
  (2) Nota, lettera, biglietto
  (3) Nota

NOTE (2)   317
(1) Résumé écrit d'un fait ou d'une
pensée destinée à faciliter la rédaction
d'un écrit ou servant d'aide-mémoire.
(2) Annotation d'un texte, généralement marginale et officieuse. *Voir*
(285) APOSTILLE.

R (1/2) записка, пометка
  (3) Нота

S (1/2/3) Nota

NUMBERING

The process of assigning and affixing a *reference number* to individual *items*. *See also* FOLIATION: STAMPING.

D Nummering
G Numerierung, Signierung
I Numerazione

COTATION 318

Opération par laquelle chaque *article* est identifié au moyen de signes (lettres, chiffres ou combinaison des deux), qui constituent la *cote*.

R [Простановка архивных шифров на единицах хранения]

S Poner signatura

NUMISMATICS

The science dealing with medals, coins and other monetary instruments and matters.

D Numismatiek, munt- en penningkunde
G Münzkunde, Numismatik
I Numismatica

NUMISMATIQUE 319

Science appliquée à l'étude des monnaies et des médailles.

R Нумизматика
S Numismática

OCR *See* OPTICAL CHARACTER RECOGNITION/READER

OFFICE FILE(S)

(1) *Documents* relating to or belonging to an office or position or connected with a person holding an office or position.
(2) *Documents* or *copies* thereof, *papers* and/or publications kept by or for officials for their private or personal use, relating directly or indirectly to their official duties. Also called convenience/personal file (US); semi-official records (UK).

D (1) –
  (2) Werkdossier
G (1) Stellenakten
  (2) Handakten
I (1) Carte d'ufficio, registratura corrente, archivio corrente

[– – –] 320

(1) *Documents* relatifs ou appartenant à un service ou à une fonction ou liés à une personne dirigeant ce service ou occupant ce poste.
(2) DOSSIER DE DOCUMENTATION *Documents* ou leur *copie* réunis par ou pour des fonctionnaires à des fins personelles et concernant plus ou moins directement l'exercice de leur fonction (Dits aussi *documents* semi-officiels, UK).

R (1/2) Дела, документы учреждения, Служебные документы
S –

OFFICIAL COPY *See* RECORD COPY

OFFICIAL RECORD
A *record (1)*, in law, having the legally recognised and judicially enforceable quality of establishing some fact.

D Akte

G Amtliches Schriftstück

I Documento ufficiale

[− − −]   321
En droit, *document* ayant légalement et juridiquement la qualité de pouvoir établir un fait quelconque.

R Официальный документ

S Documento público

OMR *See* OPTICAL CHARACTER RECOGNITION/READER

ONOMASTICS
The science dealing with the origins, form, meaning and use of names especially place-names (toponymy) and personal names (anthroponymy).

D Naamkunde, onomastiek

G Namenkunde

I Onomastica (persona), toponomastica (luogo)

ONOMASTIQUE   322
Science étudiant l'origine, la forme, la signification et l'emploi des noms, spécialement des noms de lieu (toponymie) et des noms de personne (anthroponymie).

R Ономастика

S Onomástica

OPEN FILE
(1) A *file (1)* or *(2)* to which *documents* are being added.
(2) A *file (1)* or *(2)* with no restrictions as to *access* as distinct from *closed file (2)*.

D (1/2) Open dossier

G (1) Lebendes Schriftgut, -Akten
(2) Offenes Schriftgut

I (1) Fascicolo aperto, serie aperta
(2) Documenti liberamente consultabili

(1) DOSSIER OUVERT   323
Dossier susceptible de recevoir de nouvelles *pièces*.
(2) DOSSIER COMMUNICABLE
Dossier dont la *communication* n'est pas frappée de restriction.

R (1) Дело, незаконченное делопроизводством
(2) Дело, доступное для использования

S (1) Expediente abierto
(2) Expediente accesible

OPEN RECORD GROUP
A *record group* to which future *accessions* or *accruals* are expected to be added.

FONDS OUVERT   324
Fonds susceptible d'être accru de nouveaux *documents*.

D [Niet afgesloten archiefbestand]
G [Bestand der noch Zuwachs erhält]
I Fóndo aperto, archivio aperto

R Открытый архивный фонд, комплектующийся архивный фонд
S Fondo abierto

OPERATING SYSTEM
Software which controls the operation of *computer programs* and is specific to a particular type of machine.

D Hoofdbesturingssysteem
G Betriebssystem
I Sistema operativo

SYSTEME D'EXPLOITATION   325
Logiciel destiné à la mise en oeuvre des *programmes d'ordinateur.*

R Операционная система
S Sistema operativo

OPERATIONAL VALUE *See* ADMINISTRATIVE VALUE

OPTICAL CHARACTER RECOGNITION/READER
Machine reading of manuscript or printed characters by means of light sensitive devices known as optical character readers. Both are abbreviated as OCR. When marks are similarly read, the process is known as optical mark recognition and the devices as optical mark readers (OMR).

D Optische herkenning, optische lezer
G OCR
I Riconoscimento di caratteri ottici, lettore di caratteri ottici

LECTURE OPTIQUE   326
Lecture automatique directe de caractères manuscrits ou imprimés au moyen d'un appareillage sensible à la lumière.

R (1) Распознавание оптических знаков
(2) Устройство оптического считывания

S Lector óptico

ORAL HISTORY
The results of planned interviews with individuals, usually in the form of *sound recordings* or *transcripts (3)* thereof, intended for research use.

ARCHIVES ORALES   327
Ensemble de témoignages oraux, provoqués ou spontanés, recueillis sur *disques* ou *bandes magnétiques* ou transcrits dans un but de documentation scientifique.

(continued)

D Oral history

G Mündliche Überlieferung

I Storia orale

R **Устная история**

S Archivo oral

ORDINANCE

A governmental, now especially municipal, statute or regulation.

D Verordening

G Verordnung

I Ordinanza

ORDONNANCE   328

Acte solennel et public de caractère législatif ou réglementaire.

R **Статут, положение**

S Ordenanza(s)

ORIGINAL

The initially created *document* as distinguished from any *copy* thereof.

D Origineel

G Original, Urschrift

I Originale

ORIGINAL   329

Document établi initialement par opposition à toutes ses *copies*.

R **Подлинник, оригинал**

S Original

OUTREACH PROGRAMME

Organised activities of *archives (2)* intended to acquaint potential *users* with its *holdings* and their *research value* (US). In Australia, extension service.

D —

G Öffentlichkeitsarbeit

I Programma promozionale o di diffusione

[Programme de vulgarisation]   330

Activités d'un service d'*archives (2)* destinées à faire connaître à un public potentiel l'existence et la valeur scientifique des *fonds* et *collections* qu'il conserve (US)

R **Инициативная информация архива**

S Programa de actividades culturales

OUT-LETTER

Correspondence despatched by an agency, institution or organisation and sometimes maintained in separate *series*. *See also* IN-LETTER.

D Uitgaand stuk

G Ausgang (ausgehende Schreiben), Auslauf

I Lettera spedita, missiva

CORRESPONDANCE ACTIVE   331

Copies ou *minutes* de *lettres* ou d'autres communications écrites expédiées par un organisme et parfois conservées par l'expéditeur dans une suite particulière; dite aussi courrier expédié, ou départ. *Voir aussi* (242) CORRESPON-DANCE PASSIVE.

R **Исходящий документ**

S Correspondencia

OVERSIZE DOCUMENT
A *document* too large to be boxed
or shelved in the normal manner.

D Groot formaat

G Überformatiges Dokument

I Documento fuori misura

DOCUMENT DE GRAND FORMAT 332
Document dont les dimensions
excessives exigent un conditionnement
spécial et une *conservation* à part.

R Крупноформатный документ

S Documento de gran formato

PACKING *See* BOXING

PAGE
One side of a *leaf.*

D Bladzijde, pagina

G Seite

I Pagina

PAGE 333
Un côté d'un *feuillet (2).*

R Страница

S Página

PAGINATION
(1) The act of *numbering* the
pages in a *document.*
(2) The results of this action.
See also FOLIATION.

D (1/2) Paginering

G (1/2) Paginierung

I (1/2) Paginazione

PAGINATION 334
(1) Numérotation continue des
pages d'un *document.*
(2) Résultat de cette action.
Voir aussi (195) FOLIOTAGE.

R (1/2) Пагинация

S (1/2) Paginación

PALAEOGRAPHY
The science dealing with the
development of handwriting.

D Paleografie

G Schriftkunde, Paläographie

I Palaeografia

PALÉOGRAPHIE 335
Science des anciennes écritures
manuscrites.

R Палеография

S Paleografía

PALIMPSEST
Writing material, usually *parchment,* that has been written upon
more than once; the previous
text or texts may have been
imperfectly erased, thus
remaining partly legible.

PALIMPSESTE 336
Matériau, généralement *parchemin,*
ayant successivement servi de *support*
à deux, voire à plusieurs textes, après
abrasion du précédent, les anciens textes
pouvant parfois être lus en partie ou
en totalité grâce à des procédés optiques.

(continued)

D Palimpsest
G Palimpsest
I Palinsesto

R Палимпсест
S Palimpsesto

PAPER

A *medium* made from the pulped, pressed and dried fibres of rags (woollen, linen, cotton) or from a chemical or mechanical pulp of wood or straw subsequently dried and pressed.

D Papier
G Papier
I Carta

PAPIER 337

Support d'écriture fabriqué à partir d'une pâte de fibres de chiffons (laine, lin, coton), de bois ou de paille, séchée et aplanie en forme de *feuille*.

R Бумага
S Papel

PAPERS

(1) Personal, family (and estate) *records (1)*/*archives (1)* as distinct from the *records (1)*/*archives (1)* of corporate bodies. (2) A general term used to designate more than one type of *manuscript* material (US). *See also* PERSONAL PAPERS: PRIVATE RECORDS/ARCHIVES.

D (1) Particuliere archiefbescheiden
(2) Papieren
G (1) Personen- und Familien-
papiere/-archiv(e)
(2) Papiere, Schriftgut
I (1) Archivio privato
(2) Carte

PAPIERS 338

(1) *Archives (1)* personnelles, ou *archives (1)* familiales par opposition aux *archives (1)* d'un corps constitué. (2) [Terme général désignant plusieurs types de *documents* manuscrits, US.] (3) Ensemble de *documents* non différenciés.

R (1/2) Личные, семейные,
имущест- венные документы
S (1/2) Papeles

PAPERWORK MANAGEMENT

The application of cost reduction principles and techniques to records creation, maintenance, use and *disposal*, particularly those involving *correspondence*, *forms*, directives, and *reports* (US). *See also* RECORDS MANAGEMENT.

[– – –] 339

Application des principes et des techniques de réduction des coûts à la gestion des *archives (1)* et à la simplification du travail de bureau (US).

121

(continued)

D —

G Organisation der Schriftgut-
verwaltung

I —

R Делопроизводство

S Racionalización del papelo

PAPYRUS

(1) A *medium* made from a water-
plant by the ancient Egyptians,
Greeks and Romans by soaking,
pressing, and drying thin slices
of its pith laid crosswise.
(2) A *document* on *papyrus (1)*.

D (1/2) Papyrus

G (1/2) Papyrus

I (1/2) Papiro

PAPYRUS 340

(1) *Support* d'écriture fabriqué dans
l'Antiquité et au haut Moyen âge
en Egypte, Grèce et Italie à partir
de la moelle d'une plante aquatique,
le papyrus, découpée en fines lamelles
collées en croix, pressées et séchées.
(2) *Document* écrit sur *papyrus (1)*.

R (1/2) Папирус

S (1/2) Papiro

PARCHMENT

(1) The skin of an animal, usually
a sheep or goat, prepared for
use as a writing material.
Parchment made from calf, kid
or lamb skin is called vellum.
(2) A *document* on *parchment (1)*.

D (1/2) Perkament

G (1/2) Pergament

I (1/2) Pergamena

PARCHEMIN 341

(1) Morceau de peau de mouton ou
de chèvre, parfois de veau mort-né
(vélin), spécialement apprêté pour
servir de *support* à l'écriture.
(2) *Document* écrit sur *parchemin
(1)*.

R (1/2) Пергамен

S (1/2) Pergamino

PARISH REGISTER(S)

Register(s) established and kept
by an ecclesiastical parish, recording
chronologically baptisms, marriages,
burials and possibly other *information. See also* CIVIL REGISTERS:
VITAL STATISTICS.

REGISTRE PAROISSIAL 342

Registre établi et tenu à jour par le
ministre du culte responsable d'une
paroisse ou son représentant, où
sont portés dans l'ordre chronologique les actes de baptêmes, de
mariages et de sépultures survenus
en principe dans la paroisse, et
parfois d'autres informations.
Voir aussi (83) REGISTRE
D'ÉTAT CIVIL.

(continued)

D Doop-, trouw- en begraaf-
   registers
G Kirchenbücher
I Libri parrocchiali

R Метрическая книга
S Registros parroquiales,
   libros sacramentales

PARTICULAR INSTANCE PAPERS *See* CASE PAPERS/FILES

PATRIMONIAL ARCHIVES *See* FAMILY (AND ESTATE) ARCHIVES

PERFECT BINDING *See* ADHESIVE BINDING

PERIPHERAL   PÉRIPHÉRIQUE   343

Any unit of equipment in an
automatic data processing system
separate from the *central
processing unit* which may provide the system with outside
communication.

Appareillage faisant partie d'un
ordinateur, distinct de *l'unité
centrale,* susceptible de lui être
connecté et d'être commandé
par elle.

D Randapparatuur
G Peripher
I Unità periferica

R Периферийное /внешнее/
  оборудование ЭВМ
S Periférica

PERMANENT/DURABLE PAPER   PAPIER STABLE   344

Paper with neutral or slightly
alkaline *pH value* which does
not show degradation over long
periods of time.

Terme général désignant toute
espèce de *papier* non acide ou
alcalin, ne se dégradant pas
rapidement.

D Zuurvrij papier
G Holzfreies Papier,
   Dokumentenpapier
I Carta neutra

R Долговечная бумага
S Papel permanente/durable

PERMANENT VALUE *See* ARCHIVAL VALUE

PERMANENT WITHDRAWAL   [− − −]   345

The permanent return of *documents* from the physical and
legal *custody* of *archives (2),*

Restitution faite par un service
d'archives (2) à l'administration
versante ou à son successeur, de

(continued)

to the creating agency or to its successor(s).

D [Restitutie]

G [Rückforderung auf Dauer]

I Restituzione permanente

documents ayant recouvré un nouvel intérêt administratif.

R —

S —

PERSONAL FILE *See* OFFICE FILE(S) (2): PERSONNEL FILE

PERSONAL PAPERS
The private *documents* accumulated by, belonging to and subject to the disposition of an individual person. *See also* PAPERS.

D Persoonlijke papieren

G Persönliche Papiere, Nachlaß

I Carte personali

PAPIERS PERSONNELS 346
Documents privés accumulés par un individu, lui appartenant et dont il dispose à son gré. *Voir aussi* (338) PAPIERS (1).

R Личные документы

S Documentos personales

PERSONNEL FILE
A *file (1)* maintained by an organisation for each of its employees giving personal details and *information* relating to their service. Also called personal file (UK) or staff file.

D Personeelsdossier, persoonsdossier

G Personalakte(n)

I Fascicolo personale

DOSSIER DE PERSONNEL 347
Dossier (1) tenu par un organisme pour chacun de ses employés et constitué de *pièces* relatives à leur situation personnelle et familiale, leur carrière administrative et leur manière de servir.

R Личное дело

S Expediente personal

PERTINENCE *See* FUNCTIONAL PERTINENCE: PRINCIPLE OF PERTINENCE: TERRITORIAL PERTINENCE

PETITION
A written request to an authority for the performance of specific action.

D Petitie

G Petition, Bittschrift, (*obs.:*) Supplik, Eingabe

I Petizione

PÉTITION 348
Demande écrite visant à obtenir une décision ponctuelle.

R Петиция, прошение

S Instancia

pH VALUE

A measure of the intensity of
the acid content of *paper*, also
referred to as hydrogen ion con-
centration. pH is expressed in
terms of a logarithmic scale from
0 to 14; the neutral point is 7.0,
with values above 7 alkaline,
values below, acid.

D Zuurgraad

G pH-Wert

I Grado di pH

ACIDITÉ, pH 349

Mesure du degré d'acidité que présente un *papier*, appelée aussi con-
centration de l'ion d'hydrogène;
la valeur pH est exprimée selon une
échelle logarithmique de 0 à 14;
le point neutre est 7, les valeurs
supérieures étant alcalines et les
valeurs inférieures acides.

R Степень кислотности
бумаги

S Valor pH

PHONOGRAM *See* SOUND RECORDING

PHONOTAPE

A *sound recording* on *magnetic
tape*. Also called audio-tape or
sound tape.

D Geluidsband

G Tonband

I Nastro sonoro

BANDE SONORE 350

Ruban magnétique portant
l'enregistrement d'un *document*
sonore; dit aussi audio-bande.

R Фонодокумент

S Banda sonora

PHOTOCOPY

A *copy* produced on or by means
of sensitized material by the
action of light or other radiant
energy with or without intermediate *negative*.

D Fotokopie

G Fotokopie, Photokopie

I Fotocopia

PHOTOCOPIE 351

Reproduction directe d'un
document par une machine
automatique utilisant un *papier*
sensible aux phénomènes lumineux,
chimiques ou électrostatiques, avec
ou sans *négatif* intermédiaire.

R Фотокопия

S Fotocopia

PHOTOGRAPH

An *image* produced on photo-
sensitive material by the chemical
action of light or other radiant
energy. Also called still picture.
See also NEGATIVE: POSITIVE:
PRINT(1).

PHOTOGRAPHIE 352

Image obtenue sur une surface
sensibilisée par l'intermédiaire d'une
pellicule impressionnée par l'action
de la lumière ou d'autres sources
d'énergie rayonnante. *Voir aussi*
(312) NÉGATIF, (361) COPIE
POSITIVE, (369) ÉPREUVE.

D Foto

G Fotografie, Photographie

I Fotografia

R Фотография, Фотодокумент

S Fotografía

PHOTOGRAPHIC RECORDS/ ARCHIVES

A *collection* or *accumulation* of *photographs,* including *negatives* and *prints (1)* together with related *textual records/archives.* *See also* AUDIO-VISUAL RE-CORDS/ARCHIVES: ICONO-GRAPHIC RECORDS/ARCHIVES.

D Fotoarchief

G Fotoarchiv(e)

I Archivio fotografico, collezione fotografica

ARCHIVES PHOTOGRAPHIQUES 353

Fonds ou *collections* de *photo-graphies,* incluant les *diapositives,* les *négatifs,* les *épreuves* et, le cas échéant, les *documents* s'y rapportant. *Voir aussi* (36) ARCHIVES AUDIO-VISUELLES, (230) ARCHIVES ICONOGRAPHIQUES.

R Фотодокументы

S Archivo fotográfico

PHOTOSTAT

(1) A trade name for photo-copying cameras, chemicals and sensitive materials that produce *copies* with the same *polarity* as the *original.*
(2) A *copy* produced by this process.

D (1) –
   (2) Fotokopie

G (1) –
   (2) Fotokopie, Photokopie

I (1) Apparecchiatura fotostatica
   (2) Copia fotostatica

PHOTOSTAT 354

(1) Appellation déposée d'un procédé de *reproduction* établissant des *copies* de même *polarité* que l'*original.*
(2) *Copie* établie par ce procédé.

R (1) Фотостат. Аппарат контактного копирования
   (2) Фотокопия

S (1) Fotostato
   (2) Copia fotostática

PHYSICAL CUSTODY *See* CUSTODY

PIECE

In UK usage, an *item.*

D Stuk

G (Schrift)Stück

I Pezzo, unità archivistica

[– – –] 355
Article (U.K).

R –

S Pieza

PLAN

A *document* in graphic or photogrammetric form depicting the arrangement in horizontal section of a structure, piece of ground, etc. *See also* MAP.

D Plattegrond

G Plan

I Pianta, piano, mappa

PLAN CABINET/CASE

A cabinet, usually metal, for the horizontal or vertical storage of *maps, plans, charts*, and other *oversize documents*. Also called map case.

D Kaartenkast

G Kartenschrank, Planschrank

I Porta mappe

PLANETARY CAMERA

A *microfilm* camera so constructed that the *original document* and *film* are stationary and in parallel planes during exposure. The *document* is changed manually and the *film* automatically advanced one *frame* after exposure. Also called a flatbed camera. *See also* ROTARY CAMERA: STEP-AND-REPEAT CAMERA.

D Stappencamera

G Schrittkamera

I Planetario

POLARITY

A term used to indicate the change (reversal) in or retention of the

PLAN   356

Document représentant, sous forme graphique ou photogrammétrique sur un *support* plat et, à l'époque moderne, avec une échelle inférieure au 20,000^e, une portion de terrain. *Voir aussi* (284) CARTE, (469) DESSIN TECHNIQUE.

R План

S Plano

MEUBLE À PLAN   357

Meuble de bois ou de métal destiné à la conservation horizontale ou verticale de *plans, cartes, chartes, gravures, affiches* ou autres *documents de grand format*.

R Шкаф для хранения карт и планов

S Archivador de planos

CAMÉRA STATIQUE   358

Appareil de *microfilmage* dans lequel le *document* à reproduire et le *film* sont immobiles durant l'exposition, le *document* étant placé à la main et le *film* vierge avancé manuellement ou automatiquement pour chaque nouvelle exposition. *Voir aussi* (422) CAMÉRA CINÉTIQUE.

R Микрофильмирующий аппарат статической съемки

S Cámara estática

POLARITÉ   359

Terme servant à indiquer, pour une *copie*, la modification ou le maintien

(continued)

dark to light relationship of an *image* or *copy* as compared with the *original*.

D Polariteit

G Polarität

I Polarità

du contraste entre sombre et clair, par comparaison avec l'*original*.

R Контрастность

S Polaridad

PORTFOLIO

A flat, portable case for the storage of large or fragile *documents*.

D Portefeuille

G Mappe

I Cartella

CARTON À DESSIN 360

Portefeuille rigide formé de deux plats de carton reliés par un dos souple, munis de rabats et de cordons, servant à conserver des *documents de grand format* ou fragiles. Parfois dit *portefeuille* (147).

R [Папка для крупноформатных или ветхих документов]

S Carpeta

POSITIVE

A photographic *image* having the same *polarity* as the *original*.

D Positief

G Positiv(kopie)

I Positivo

COPIE POSITIVE 361

Photographie ou *copie* ayant la même *polarité* que le *document* reproduit ou, si elles sont colorées, les mêmes valeurs tonales.

R Позитив

S Positivo

POSITIVE MICROFILM

A *microfilm* consisting of *positive images*.

D Positieve microfilm

G Positiv(mikro)film

I Microfilm positivo

MICROFILM POSITIF 362

Microfilm composé d'*images* positives.

R Позитивный микрофильм

S Microfilme positivo

POSTER

A *document* usually printed on one side of a single *sheet* of *paper* and often illustrated, posted to advertise or publicise something. Also called a placard.

AFFICHE 363

Document rédigé à des fins d'information ou de publicité, généralement imprimé d'un seul côté d'une *feuille* de *papier,* souvent illustré, et destiné à être exposé dans un lieu public. Parfois appelé placard.

(continued)

D Affiche, aanplakbilijet

G Plakat

I Manifesto

R Плакат, афиша

S Cartel

PRELIMINARY INVENTORY *See* INVENTORY

PRESERVATION

(1) A basic archival function of storing and protecting *records (1)* / *archives (1)*.
(2) The totality of processes and operations involved in the physical protection of *records (1)* / *archives (1)* against damage or deterioration and in the *restoration/repair* of damaged or deteriorated *documents*.

D (1) Bewaring
   (2) Conservering

G (1) Aufbewahrung, Verwahrung
   (2) Konservierung

I (1) Preservazione, salvaguarda
   (2) Protezione e restauro

(1) CONSERVATION (2) 364

Fonction fondamentale des *archives (2)* consistant à assurer l'emmagasinage et la protection des *archives (1)*.

(2) PRÉSERVATION
Ensemble des procédés et des mesures destinés à assurer d'une part la protection physique des *archives (1)* contre tous les agents de détérioration, d'autre part la remise en état des *documents* endommagés.

R (1) Хранение архивных
   документов
   (2) Обеспечение физико-
   химической сохранности
   архивных документов

S (1) Conservación
   (2) Preservación

PRESERVATION LABORATORY *See* RESTORATION LABORATORY

PRESERVATION MICROFILMING

The use of *microfilm* to preserve the informational content of *documents* that either are in poor condition or that were created utilising poor quality materials, as well as to preserve *originals* from deterioration through repeated handling and use. *See also* SECURITY MICROFILMING: DISPOSAL MICROFILMING.

D Substitutieverfilming (ter bescherming van het origineel)

G Ersatzverfilmung (aus Konservierungsgründen)

I Microfilmatura di preservazione

MICROFILMAGE DE PRÉSERVATION 365

Microfilmage effectué soit pour préserver le contenu de *documents* détériorés physiquement, soit pour prévenir la détérioration d'*originaux* résultant de communications trop fréquentes.

R Микрофильмирование в целях создания страхового фонда документов

S Microfilme de preservación

PRINCIPLE OF PERTINENCE

A principle, now rejected, for the *arrangement* of *archives (1)* in terms of their subject content regardless of their *provenance* and original order.

D Pertinentiebeginsel

G Pertinenzprinzip

I Principio di pertinenza, ordinamento per materia

[Principe de pertinence]   36

Principe de *classement,* désormais abandonné, selon lequel les *archives (1)* étaient regroupées par sujets, sans tenir compte ni de leur *provenance,* ni de leur *classement* primitif ou d'origine.

R Принцип пертиненции

S Principio temático

PRINCIPLE OF PROVENANCE

The basic principle that *records (1)/ archives (1)* of the same *provenance (1)* must not be intermingled with those of any other *provenance (1);* frequently referred to as 'respect des fonds'. Also extended to include the *registry principle.*

D Herkomstbeginsel, bestemmingsbeginsel

G Provenienzprinzip

I Principio di provenienza

PRINCIPE DU RESPECT DES FONDS/
PRINCIPE DE PROVENANCE   367

Principe fondamental selon lequel les *archives (1)* d'une même *provenance* ne doivent pas être mélangées à celles d'une autre *provenance;* dit aussi principe de provenance; ce principe inclut parfois le *principe de respect de l'orde primitif* (404).

R Принцип происхождения [провениенцпринцип]

S Principio de procedencia

PRINCIPLE OF RESPECT FOR ARCHIVAL STRUCTURE

The principle that the methodology used in archival operations, particularly *appraisal, arrangement* and *description,* should reflect the varying forms and structures of the *records (1) /archives (1)* and their administrative and functional contents. *See also* REGISTRY PRINCIPLE.

D Structuurbeginsel

G Strukturprinzip

I Principio del rispetto della struttura archivistica originaria

PRINCIPE DU RESPECT DE LA STRUCTURE ARCHIVISTIQUE   3

Principe selon lequel un *fonds d'archives* doit conserver ou recevoir un *classement* correspondant aux structures administratives internes de l'organisme qui l'a créé. *Voir aussi* (404) PRINCIPE DU RESPECT DE L'ORDRE PRIMITIF.

R [Структурный признак систематизации]

S Principio de respeto a la estructura

130

PRINT

(1) A *copy* of a *photograph,* especially one made from a *negative.*
(2) A picture or design printed from a plate, block, roll in the form of an etching, woodcut, lithograph, including both proofs and final versions.

D (1) Afdruk
  (2) Prent

G (1) Abzug
  (2) Druck, Stich

I (1) Stampa
  (2) Prova d'autore, stampa

(1) ÉPREUVE 369

Copie photographique, en particulier le positif tiré d'un *négatif.*
(2) ESTAMPE
Tirage d'essai ou définitif sur *papier* d'une planche gravée ou d'un texte imprimé.

R (1) Фотокопия, позитив
  (2) Гравюра, Литография, офорт

S (1) Fotografía
  (2) Impresión

PRINTED ARCHIVES

(1) The totality of printed or processed publications or *documents* of an agency, institution or organisation transferred to *archives (2).*
(2) All printed or processed *archives (1)* in the custody of *archives (2).*

D (1/2) Gedrukte archivalia

G (1) (Amts)Drucksachen
  (2) (Amts)Drucksachen-Abteilung

I (1/2) Raccolta delle publica-
       zione ufficiali, archivi
       stampati

ARCHIVES IMPRIMÉES 370

(1) Ensemble des *documents* imprimés ou multigraphiés produits par une institution pour les nécessités de son fonctionnement.
(2) Toutes les *archives (1)* imprimées conservées dans un service d'*archives (2).*

R (1/2) Печатные материалы учреждений, архива

S (1/2) Archivo de impresos

PRINTOUT

The output of a *computer* in printed form.

D Printout

G Ausdruck

I Tabulato

LISTING 371

Sortie d'*ordinateur* sous forme imprimée.

R Табуляграмма

S Salida impresa de ordenador

PRIVACY

The right to be secure from unauthorised disclosure of

RESPECT DE LA VIE PRIVÉE 372

Droit garantissant les individus contre la divulgation des informa-

information contained in *records (1)* / *archives (1)* relating to personal and private matters.

D Recht op privacy, recht op bescherming van de personlijke levenssfeer

G Persönlichkeitsschutz

I Riservatezza

tions d'ordre personnel ou privé les concernant contenues dans les *archives (1)*.

R [Обеспечение тайны архивной информации, касающейся частных лиц]

S Privacidad

PRIVATE PAPERS *See* PERSONAL PAPERS

PRIVATE RECORDS/ARCHIVES
Records (1)/ *archives (1)* of nongovernmental agencies, institutions and organisations and/or of non-governmental *provenance (1)*. *See also* FAMILY (AND ESTATE) ARCHIVES.

D Particuliere archiefbescheiden

G Privatarchiv(e)

I Documenti/archivi privati; documenti/archive pubblici di enti non statali

ARCHIVES PRIVÉES   373
Archives (1) soit d'individus ou de familles, soit d'institutions ou d'organisations non publiques, ou de *provenance* non publique.

R —

S Documentos/archivos privados

PROCEEDINGS
A *record (1)* of business transacted at a meeting or conference. Also called transactions.

D Verslag

G Protokoll, Verhandlungs-, Sitzungsbericht

I Verbale, processo verbale, protocollo, atti

REGISTRE DE DÉLIBÉRATIONS   374
Enregistrement des affaires traitées lors d'une réunion, d'une conférence.

R Протокол совещания

S Acta

PROCESSING
(1) A collective term comprising recording *acquisitions, arrangement, description* and *preservation* of *records (1)* / *archives (1)*.
(2) The treatment of exposed

(1) TRAITEMENT   375
Terme collectif recouvrant le *versement*, la *conservation*, le *tri*, le *classement* et l'*inventaire* des *archives (1)*.
(2) DÉVELOPPEMENT

(continued)

photographic material to make
the latent *image*(s) visible.
See also AUTOMATIC DATA
PROCESSING.

D (1) [Bewerking]
   (2) Ontwikkelen

G (1) Bearbeitung
   (2) Entwicklung

I (1) Conservazione
   (2) Sviluppo

Traitement de matériaux photographiques impressionnés, en vue
de faire apparaître l'*image*
latente.

R (1) [Прием, научно-техни-
ческая обработка, хране-
ние архивных документов
и создание к ним инфор-
мационных средств]
(2) Проявление фотопленки

S (1) Tratamiento
   (2) Revelado

PRODUCTION

The temporary removal of an *item*
form its place of storage for use.
See also CHARGE OUT : LOAN.

COMMUNICATION   376

Objectif fondamental de tout service d'*archives (2)* consistant à
mettre, pour une durée limitée, des
documents à la disposition des
lecteurs administratifs ou scientifiques soit sur place, soit avec déplacement dans une autre institution
(*communication avec déplacement*).
Voir aussi (73,1) FICHE DE
DÉPLACEMENT, (270) COMMUNI-
CATION AVEC DÉPLACEMENT.

D Lichten, uitlichten

G Aushebung, Vorlage

I Estrazione, riassunzione

R —

S Prestamo

PRODUCTION TICKET

A *document,* signed by a *user*
to request an *item* for use.

BULLETIN DE DEMANDE   377

Formulaire rempli et signé par un
lecteur pour demander *communication* d'un *article* aux fins de consultation.

D Aanvraagbriefje

G Bestellschein, -zettel

I Scheda di richiesta

R Требование на выдачу
документов

S Papeleta de pedido

PROGRAM *See* COMPUTER PROGRAM

PROGRAMME RECORDS

Records (1) relating to the
substantive functions of an agency,

[– – –]   378

Documents créés par une institution
dans l'exercice de ses attributions, par

i.e. the programme for which it is
responsible, as distinct from
housekeeping records.

D [Archiefbescheiden betreffende de taak van het overheids-
orgaan]

G Fachschriftgutachten, Fachakten;
Schriftgut der Aufgabenverwal-
tung

I —

opposition aux *documents* de gestion
interne.

R [Документы по основной
деятельности учреждения]

S —

PROJECT FILE *See* CASE PAPERS/FILES

PROTOCOL

(1) A formal *document* embodying
the terms of a legal transaction.
(2) A diplomatic *document* especially the final text of a treaty or
compact, signed by the negotia-
tors and subject to subsequent
ratification.

D (1) Akte
(2) Protocol

G (1) Protokoll
(2) Unterhändler-Urkunde

I (1) –
(2) Protocollo diplomatico

[– – –]   379

(1) *Document* formel dans lequel
sont incorporés les termes d'une
transaction légale.
(2) PROTOCOLE
Document diplomatique, plus particulièrement le texte final d'un traité
ou d'un *contrat* signé par les négocia-
teurs et sujet à ratification ultérieure.

R (1) Юридический акт
(2) [Проект дипломатичес-
кого документа]

S (1) Contrato
(2) Protocolo

PROVENANCE

(1) The agency, institution,
organisation or individual that
created, accumulated and maintained *records (1) / archives (1)*
in the conduct of its business
prior to their transfer to a
records centre/archives (3).
(2) In manuscript terminology,
any source from which *personal
papers* or *manuscripts* are
acquired. *See also* FUNCTIONAL
PROVENANCE: PRINCIPLE OF

PROVENANCE   380

(1) Institution, administration,
établissement, organisme ou personne privée qui a créé, accumulé
et conservé des *documents d'archives (1)* au cours de la conduite de
ses affaires avant le transfert à un
centre de préarchivage ou à un service d'*archives (2). Voir aussi* (367)
PRINCIPE DU RESPECT DES
FONDS, (471) PROVENANCE
TERRITORIALE.
(2) Quand il s'agit de *manuscrits*

(continued)

PROVENANCE: TERRITORIAL
PROVENANCE.

D (1) Archiefvormende instantie
(2) Herkomst

G (1) Provenienz(stelle),
Registraturbildner
(2) Provenienz

I (1/2) Provenienza

ou d'*archives (1)* personnelles: la
source dont ils proviennent.

R (1/2) **Фондообразователь**

S (1/2) Procedencia

PUBLIC RECORDS/ARCHIVES
Records (1)/archives (1) legally
defined as public; also used to
designate *records (1)/archives (1)*
open to public inspection.

D Openbare archiefbescheiden

G Öffentliches Schriftgut/
Archivgut

I Documenti/archivi pubblici;
documenti/archivi consultabili

ARCHIVES PUBLIQUES 381
Archives (1) définies par la loi
comme publiques; terme parfois
utilisé pour désigner les *archives (1)*
consultables par le public.

R **Документы государствен-
ных учреждений**

S Documentos/archivos públicos

PULPING *See* MACERATION

PUNCH(ED) CARD/TAPE
A *paper* card or *tape* on which
data (1) are recorded by the
punching of holes in specified
positions in accordance with a
predesignated *code (1)*
usually machine-readable.

D Ponskaart, ponsband

G Lochkarte, -streifen

I Scheda perforata, nastro
perforato

CARTE OU BANDE PERFORMÉE 382
Carte ou *bande* où sont enregistrées
sous forme de perforations codées
des informations généralement
lisibles par machine.

R **Перфокарта, перфолента**

S Ficha perforada, cinta
perforada

PURGING *See* WEEDING

QUARTZ LAMP *See* ULTRA-VIOLET LAMP

QUESTIONED DOCUMENTS
Documents whose authenticity
has been challenged.

D [Stukken beticht van
valsheid]

G Dokumente von zweifelhafter
Echtheit

I Documenti di dubbia
autenticità

QUIRE *See* SIGNATURE (2)

RACKING *See* SHELVING

RANGE *See* ROW

READER *See* USER

READER/MICROFORM READER
An optical device for viewing a
projected and enlarged *micro-image*.

D (Microfilm)leesapparaat

G (Mikrofilm-/Mikrofiche-)
Lesegerät

I Lettore microimmagini

READER-PRINTER
A machine which combines the
functions of a *reader/microform
reader* and an *enlarger-printer*.

D Reader-printer

G Lese- und Rückvergrößerungs-
gerät

I Lettore-stampatore

DOCUMENTS SUSPECTS
Documents dont l'authenticité
a été contestée.

R [Документы, подлинность
которых вызывает сом-
нение]

S Documentos dudosos

APPAREIL DE LECTURE/
LECTEUR DE MICROFORMES
Appareil de lecture permettant,
par leur projection agrandie, la
lecture de *micro-images*.

R Читательный аппарат

S Aparato lector

LECTEUR-REPRODUCTEUR DE
MICROCOPIES
Appareil permettant à la fois la
lecture et la *reproduction* automatique et agrandie d'une *micro-image*.

R Читально-копировальный
аппарат

S Aparato lector-impresor

READER'S CARD/TICKET

A *document,* issued by *archives (2)* granting permission to a *user* to consult *records (1)* / *archives (1)* during a specified period.

D [Lezerskaart]

G Benutzerkarte, -ausweis

I Tessera di ammissione

CARTE DE LECTEUR   386

Carte délivrée par un service d'*archives* (2), accordant à son titulaire l'autorisation de consulter des *archives* (1) durant sa période de validité.

R **Читательский билет для исследователей**

S Tarjeta de investigador

READING FILE *See* CHRONOLOGICAL FILE

READING ROOM *See* SEARCH ROOM

RECORDS(S)

(1) Recorded *information* (*document*(s)) regardless of form or *medium* created, received and maintained by an agency, institution, organisation or individual in pursuance of its legal obligations or in the transaction of business.
See also OFFICIAL RECORD.
(2) In *automatic data processing,* a unit of *data (1)* forming the basic element of a *file (3)* and consisting in turn of a number of inter-related data fields.

D (1) Archiefbescheiden, archiefstukken
(2) Record

G (1) Registraturgut, Schriftgut
(2) Datensatz

I (1) Archivio
(2) Record, unità informativa

(1) DOCUMENTS D'ARCHIVES   387

Documents contenant une information quels que soient leur date, leur forme et leur *support* matériel, produits ou reçus par toute personne physique ou morale, et par tout service ou organisme public ou privé, dans l'exercice de leur activité.
(2) ENREGISTREMENT
En *informatique,* ensemble de *données (1)* apparentées, traité comme un tout.

R (1) **документы, документальный фонд**
(2) **Запись информации**

S (1/2) Documento(s)

RECORD COPY

That *copy* of a *document* that is placed on file as the official copy. Also referred to as a file copy.

D Archiefexemplaar

G Exemplum

I Copia autentica ad uso interno

EXEMPLAIRE DE RÉFÉRENCE   388

Copie d'un *document* placé dans un *dossier* et tenant lieu de *copie* officielle.

R **Копия документа**

S Copia oficial, traslado oficial

RECORD GROUP

A body of organisationally and functionally related *records (1)* established on the basis of *provenance (1)* with particular regard to the administrative history, complexity and quantity of the *records (1)/archives (1)* of the agency, institution or organisation involved (US). *See also* ARCHIVE GROUP: COLLECTIVE RECORD GROUP: FONDS: GENERAL RECORD GROUP: MANUSRIPT GROUP: SUB-GROUP.

D Archief

G Bestand

I Fondo, archivio

[SERIE (2)]

Ensemble d'*archives* (1) ayant entre elles un lien organisationnel et fonctionnel, classé conformement au *principe de respect des fonds,* en tenant compte de l'histoire administrative, de la structure et de l'importance quantitative des archives de l'institution concernée, US].

R Архивный фонд учреждения

S Serie

RECORD OFFICE *See* ARCHIVES (2)

RECORD SERIES *See* SERIES

RECORD SUB-GROUP *See* SUB-GROUP

RECORDS ADMINISTRATION *See* RECORDS MANAGEMENT

RECORDS ADMINISTRATOR *See* RECORDS MANAGER

RECORDS CENTRE

A building, usually specially designed and constructed, for the low-cost storage, maintenance and *communication* of *semi-current records* pending their ultimate *disposal.* Also called intermediate repository or limbo. In US, *current records* are also stored in a records centre.

D Tussenarchief, tussendepot

G Zwischenarchiv

I Prearchivio, archivio intermedio

CENTRE / DÉPÔT DE PRÉARCHIVAGE / DÉPÔT INTERMÉDIAIRE

Service d'*archives* (2) spécialisé dans la *conservation* et la *communication* des *archives intermédiaires.*

R —

S Archivo intermedio

RECORDS CENTRE CARTON/
CONTAINER
  A corrugated cardboard *box*
  designed to hold one cubic foot
  of *records (1)* and used chiefly in
  records centres (US).

  D Archiefdoos

  G Zwischenarchiv-Karton

  I Contenitore, scatola, busta

[– – –]   **391**
  Carton d'un pied cube utilisé dans
  les *centres de préarchivage* pour
  contenir des *archives (1)* (U.S.)

  R –

  S Caja

RECORDS CONTROL SCHEDULE *See* RECORDS SCHEDULE

RECORDS CREATION *See* RECORDS MANAGEMENT

RECORDS DISPOSAL *See* DISPOSAL.

RECORDS DISPOSAL SCHEDULE *See* RECORDS SCHEDULE

RECORDS MAINTENANCE AND USE *See* RECORDS MANAGEMENT

RECORDS MANAGEMENT
  That area of general administrative
  management concerned with achiev-
  ing economy and efficiency in the
  creation, maintenance, use and
  disposal of *records (1)*, i.e. during
  their entire life cycle. *See also*
  PAPERWORK MANAGEMENT.

  D Registratuur, post- en
     archiefzaken

  G [Organisation der Informations-
     träger-/Schriftgutverwaltung]

  I Gestione dei documenti

GESTION DES DOCUMENTS   **392**
  Terme utilisé au Canada franco-
  phone pour désigner l'ensemble
  des mesures visant à l'économie
  et à l'efficacité dans la création,
  le *tri*, la *conservation* et l'utilisation des *archives (1)*,
  correspondant au terme
  américain 'records management'.

  R Делопроизводство

  S Gestión de documentos

RECORDS MANAGER
  A person professionally occupied
  in the conduct of a *records
  management* programme. Also
  known as a records officer or a
  records administrator.

[– – –]   **393**
  Spécialiste de la mise en oeuvre des
  programmes de *gestion des documents*.

(continued)

D Registrator

G [(Schriftgut-) Organisator],
   Registrator

I Protocollista

R Организатор делопроиз-
   водства

S —

RECORDS RETIREMENT *See* DISPOSAL

RECORDS RETENTION SCHEDULE *See* RECORDS SCHEDULE

RECORDS SCHEDULE

A *document* describing the recurring *records (1)* of an agency,
institution or administrative unit,
specifying those *records (1)* to be
preserved as having *archival value*
and authorising on a continuing
basis and after the lapse of specified
retention periods or the occurrence
of specified actions or events, the
destruction of the remaining
records (1). Also called comprehensive records schedule, disposal
schedule, records retention schedule,
records disposition schedule, retention
schedule, transfer schedule (US). In
UK called disposal list. *See also*
GENERAL RECORDS SCHEDULE.

D [Lijst van voor vernietiging
   vatbare en van te bewaren
   archiefbescheiden]

G Schriftgutkatalog,
   Aussonderungsrichtlinien

I Massimario di conservazione
   e/o di scarto

TABLEAU DE TRI   394

Document décrivant les *archives (1)*
d'une administration, d'un service,
ou d'une institution, indiquant les
documents à conserver en raison
de leur *valeur archivistique* et donnant
autorisation permanente d'éliminer les
autres *documents* soit après des délais
précis, soit dans des circonstances
déterminées.

R Перечни документов учреждений с указанием сроков
   хранения документов; Перечень документов, под-
   лежащих передаче на го-
   сударственное хранение

S Cuadro de selección

RECORDS SURVEY

A survey involving the gathering of
basic *information* regarding the
quantity, physical form and type,
location, physical condition, storage
facilities, rate of accumulation, uses
and similar data for the purpose of

[— — —]   395

Enquête réunissant des informations
essentielles sur la quantité, la forme et
le type physique, la localisation, la
condition physique, les conditions de
conservation, le taux d'*accroissement*
et l'utilisation de *documents* non encore
versés, ainsi que des données similaires,

(continued)

planning, *acquisition* and *disposal* programmes, microfilming operations, new facilities and related archival activities.

en vue de la planification, des programmes d'*accroissement* et d'*élimination,* des opérations de *microfilmage,* des programmes d'équipement et d'autres activités archivistiques.

D Inspectierapport

G [Organisationsprüfung der Informationsträger-/ Schriftgutverwaltung]

I Censimento archivistico

R —

S —

REDUCTION RATIO
A measure of the number of times a given linear dimension of a *document* is reduced when photographed, expressed as e.g. 12X, 14X, 16X.

D Verkleinigsfactor

G Verkleinerungsgrad

I Rapporto/fattore di riduzione

TAUX DE RÉDUCTION   396
Terme exprimant en chiffres le degré de réduction photographique d'un *document.*

R Краткость

S Indice de reducción

REEL
(1) A *microfilm, motion picture, film* or *magnetic tape roll* carrier consisting of a circular core and two circular flanges.
(2) A *roll* of *microfilm, motion picture film* or *magnetic tape* on such a carrier.

D (1) Spoel
    (2) Rol

G (1) Spule
    (2) (Film)Rolle

I (1) Bobina
    (2) Microfilm, Bobina

(1) BOBINE   397
Cylindre muni à ses extrémités de deux disques perpendiculaires à son axe, autour duquel sont enroulés des *films,* des *microfilms,* ou des *bandes magnétiques.*
(2) ROULEAU (1)
Microfilm, film cinématographique ou *bande magnétique* enroulé sur une *bobine.*

R (1/2) Сердечник, бобина

S (1) Carrete
    (2) Rollo

REFERENCE MICROFILMING
The use of *microfilm* to facilitate *reference service.*

MICROFILMAGE DE COMMUNICATION
Microfilmage effectué pour   398
faciliter la consultation de *documents.*

(continued)

D [Verfilming voor de gebruiker]

G Verfilmung für Benutzungszwecke

I Microfilmatura di consultazione

R Микрофильмирование: текущего использования

S Microfilme de consulta

REFERENCE NUMBER

The unique number assigned to an *item* to facilitate its storage and retrieval.

COTE   399

Chiffre(s), lettre(s) ou combinaison des deux choisis suivant un système alphanumérique ou décimal et affecté(s), dans un service d'*archives (2)* donné, à un *document* ou à un *article* pour l'identifier et en faciliter le rangement ou le repérage.

D Nummer

G Signatur, Aktenzeichen

I Segnatura

R Архивный шифр

S Signatura

REFERENCE ROOM *See* INVENTORY ROOM

REFERENCE SERVICE

The activities involved in providing *information* about or from *records (1)/archives (1)*, making *holdings* available for use in *search rooms* and providing *copies* or *reproductions.*

SERVICE DES RENSEIGNEMENTS   400

Dans les *archives (2),* service chargé d'informer les *chercheurs* sur la nature des *documents* conservés dans le service selon le ou les thèmes choisis, sur les conditions de leur *communicabilité,* sur les *instruments de recherche* permettant de les identifier et sur les moyens d'en obtenir *communication* et / ou *reproduction.*

D Inlichtingendienst

G Benutzerdienst

I Servizio di informazione

R Научно-информационное обслуживание

S Servicio de información

REGIONAL ARCHIVES

Archives (2) of the intermediate levels of government as distinguished from *central archives* and *local archives (2).*

ARCHIVES RÉGIONALES   401

Archives (2) des niveaux intermédiaires de l'administration publique, différentes des *archives centrales* et des archives locales.

D Regionale archieven

G Regionalarchiv(e)

I Archivio regionale, archivio provinciale

R —

S Archivo regional

REGISTER

A *document,* usually a *volume,* in which regular *entry* is made of *data (1)* of any kind by statutory authority or because the *data (1)* are considered of sufficient importance to be exactly and formally registered.

D Register

G Amtsbuch, Geschäftsbuch

I Registro (not in volume form)

REGISTRE 402

(1) *Document,* généralement sous forme de *volume* relié, contenant l'inscription régulière d'informations homogènes en ordre soit chronologique, soit alphabétique.
(2) *Document d'archives (1)* sous forme de *volume.*

R Актовая книга

S Registro

REGISTRY

A unit of an agency, institution or organisation responsible for the creation, control and maintenance of current *files (1)/ records (1)* and/or *semi-current records.* A registry may exist at varying levels, e.g. central, departmental.

D Registratuurafdeling, algemene secretarie, afdeling post- en archiefzaken

G Registratur

I Ufficio di protocollo, registratura

BUREAU DES ARCHIVES COURANTES

Bureau d'une administration ou 403 d'une institution responsable de la création, du contrôle et de la *conservation* des *dossiers (1)* d'affaires courantes. *Voir aussi* (115) ARCHIVES COURANTES.

R Канцелярия, общий отдел учреждения, управление делами министерства, ведомства

S Registro

REGISTRY PRINCIPLE

The principle that *archives (1)* of a single *provenance (1)* should retain the arrangement established by the creating agency, institution or organisation in order to preserve existing relationships and

PRINCIPE DU RESPECT DE 404 L'ORDRE PRIMITIF

Principe de théorie archivistique selon lequel les *archives (1)* d'une même *provenance* doivent conserver le *classement* établi par l'organisme d'origine; principe parfois implicite

reference numbers; sometimes implied in the *principle of provenance* and also called the *principle of respect for original order.*

D Behoud van de oude orde

G Registraturprinzip

I Principio della registratura

dans le *principe du respect des fonds*; dit aussi principe de 'Registratur'.

R –

S Principio del orden de procedencia

REGISTRY SYSTEM
A system controlling the creation and maintenance of current *files (1)/records (1)* and/or *semi-current records* through the use of formal *registers, lists, indexes* and/or *filing plans/systems. See also* REGISTRY.

D Registratuursysteem

G Registratursystem

I Sistema di registratura

REGISTRATURE / 'REGISTRATUR' 405
Système permettant de contrôler la création et le maintien en état des *dossiers* courants au moyen de *registres, répertoires, index* et de *plans de rangement,* en usage dans les pays de tradition germanique et certains pays anglo-saxons et slaves. *Voir aussi* (115) ARCHIVES COURANTES, (403) BUREAU DES ARCHIVES COURANTES.

R [Централизованная система делопроизводства]

S –

REHABILITATION *See* RESTORATION

REINTEGRATION
The replacement in their proper place of *documents* which have been misplaced, have strayed from or been removed from their original place.

D [Terugbrengen]

G Wiedereingliederung

I Reintegrazione, reinserimento

RÉINTÉGRATION 406
Remise à leur place de *documents* déplacés ou égarés.

R –

S Reincorporación

REMOVED ARCHIVES
Archives (1) that have been removed from official *custody*

ARCHIVES DÉPLACÉES 407
Archives (1) transférées hors du service chargé officiellement de leur

(continued)

or from the country in which they were originally accumulated. Also incorrectly called fugitive archives. *See also* CONFLICTING ARCHIVAL CLAIMS.

D [Verwijderde archiefbescheiden]

G [Verlagerte(s) Archive/ Archivgut]

I Archivi asportati

conservation, ou du pays où elles se trouvaient originellement. *Voir aussi* (105) CONTENTIEUX ARCHIVISTIQUE.

R Перемещенные архивные документы

S Archivo(s) desplazado(s)

RENT ROLL *See* RENTAL

RENTAL

A *document* in which the owner of a landed estate lists all properties forming part of his estate and the rents he may expect to receive from each. Also called rent-roll.

D Legger

G Urbar, Zinsregister

I Cabreo, censuario, urbario

CENSIER, RENTIER   408

Document, souvent *registre,* dans lequel un propriétaire foncier fait inscrire le relevé de ses biens domaniaux et les cens et rentes y afférant.

R Урбарий. Переписные книги

S Censal, libro de censos, libro de rentas

REPAIR *See* RESTORATION

REPAIR ROOM/SHOP/WORKSHOP *See* RESTORATION LABORATORY

REPERTORY *See* INVENTORY

REPLEVIN

The recovery of *records (1)* / *archives (1)* by an agency institution, organisation or individual claiming ownership thereof.

D Terugvordering van archiefbescheiden

RECOUVREMENT D'ARCHIVES   409

Récupération d'*archives (1)* par l'administration, l'institution ou la personne qui en réclame la propriété. *Voir aussi* (19) ALIÉNATION.

R [Возвращение архивных документов владельцем]

(continued)

G Rückforderung, Rückgewinnung
(von entfremdetem Archivgut)

I Recupero, rivendicazione,
rivendica

S Recuperación

REPORT

A *document* containing a presentation of facts or the record of
some proceeeding, investigation,
event.

D Rapport

G Bericht

I Rapporto, atto, verbale,
processo verbale

RAPPORT 410

Document contenant l'exposé,
officiel ou non, notamment de
faits, de projets, d'enquêtes, de
procès-verbaux.

R Отчет, доклад

S Informe

REPORTS MANAGEMENT

The application of *records
management* principles and
techniques to *reports* (US).

D –

G [Organisation des Berichts-
wesens]

S –

[– – –] 411

Application des principes et des
techniques de la *gestion de documents* aux *rapports* et aux
procès-verbaux.

R –

S –

REPOSITORY *See* ARCHIVES (3): STACKS

REPRODUCTION

An exact *copy* of a *document*
in content and form but not
necessarily in size and appearance.
See also FACSIMILE.

D Reproduktie

G Reproduktion

I Riproduzione

REPRODUCTION 412

Copie exacte d'un *document* dans
son contenu et sa forme, mais pas
nécessairement dans ses dimensions.

R Репродукция, факсимиле

S Reproducción

REPROGARAPHICS/REPROGRAPHY

All copying processes including
micrographics using any form of

REPROGRAPHIE 413

Ensemble des procédés de *copie*
ou de *microcopie* par énergie rayon-

radiant energy and all duplication and office printing processes including operations connected with such processes.

D Reprografie

G Reprographie

I Reprografia

nante. Également: ensemble des procédés de duplication et d'impression utilisés dans les bureaux.

R Репрография

S Reprografía

REQUISITION *See* CHARGE OUT: PRODUCTION

RESEARCH ROOM *See* SEARCH ROOM

RESEARCH TOOL *See* FINDING AID

RESEARCH VALUE *See* INFORMATIONAL VALUE

RESEARCHER *See* USER

RESOLUTION

POUVOIR SÉPARATEUR 414

A measure of sharpness of an *image* expressed as the number of lines per millimetre discernible thereon.

D Resolutie

G Auflösung

I Potere risolvente

Mesure de la netteté d'une *image* exprimée en nombre de lignes discernables par millimètre.

R Разрешающая способность, резкость

S Resolución

RESPECT DES FONDS *See* PRINCIPLE OF PROVENANCE

RESTORATION

RESTAURATION 415

The specific measures taken for the rehabilitation and reinforcement of damaged or deteriorated *documents*. Also referred to as repair.

D Restauratie

G Restaurierung

I Restauro

Mesures spécifiques prises pour remettre en état et renforcer les *documents* endommagés.

R Реставрация

S Restauración

RESTORATION LABORATORY
That unit of a *records centre/ archives (3)* in which the processes of *restoration* are carried out. Also called preservation laboratory: repair room/shop/workshop.

D Restauratieatelier

G Restaurierungswerkstatt

I Laboratorio di restauro

ATELIER DE RESTAURATION 416
Laboratoire d'un service d'*archives (2)* où sont exécutés les travaux de *restauration*.

R Лаборатория реставрации документов

S Taller de restauración

RESTORATION OF ORIGINAL ORDER
The application of the *registry principle* in cases where the arrangement of *records (1)/ archives (1)* established by the agency, institution, organisation or individual responsible for their accumulation has been disturbed.

D Herstel van de oude orde

G Wiederherstellung der ursprünglichen (registraturmäßigen) Ordnung

I Ripristino della disposizione originaria o dell' ordine originario

RÉTABLISSEMENT DE L'ORDRE 417
Application du *principe du respect de l'ordre primitif* lorsqu'a été modifié le *classement* établi dans les *archives (1)* par l'administration, l'organisme ou l'individu producteur.

R Восстановление первоначального порядка систематизации документов

S Reordenación

RESTRICTED ACCESS
A limitation on *access* to *records(1)/ archives (1)* or to individual *documents* or to *information* of a specified type, imposed by general or specific regulations determining *access date* or general exclusions from *access. See also* SECURITY CLASSIFICATION.

D Beperkte openbaarheid

G Benutzungsbeschränkung, Sperrung

I Limitazione della consultabilità

RESTRICTION DE COMMUNICABILITÉ
Limitation d'*accès* aux *archives (1)* 418 imposée par une réglementation déterminant des délais de *communication* spécifiques ou des interdictions générales.

R Ограничение доступа к документам

S Consulta restringida

RETENTION PERIOD

The length of time, usually based upon an estimate of the frequency of current and future use, that *records (1)* should be retained in offices before they are transferred to a *records centre,* or if in a *records centre* before they are transferred to *archives (3)* or otherwise disposed of.

D Dynamische periode

G Aufbewahrungsfrist

I   Periodo minimo obbligatori di permanenza dei documenti presso l'ufficio produttore

DÉLAI DE CONSERVATION DANS LES BUREAUX   419

Durée variable, généralement fondée sur la fréquence d'utilisation courante ou future, pendant laquelle les *documents* sont maintenus dans leur organisme d'origine avant leur versement dans un *centre de pré-archivage* ou dans un service *d'archives (2)* ou avant qu'il en soit disposé autrement.

R Сроки, период хранения документов в архивах учреждений

S Periodo de retención

RETENTION PLAN/SCHEDULE *See* RECORDS SCHEDULE

RETIREMENT *See* DISPOSAL

REVERSAL FILM

A *film* in which the originally formed latent *negative image* is converted during *processing (2)* directly to a *positive image* on the same basis.

D Omkeerfilm

G Umkehrfilm

I   Pellicola autopositiva

FILM INVERSIBLE   420

Film dans lequel l'*image négative* latente est directement transformée durant le traitement en une *image positive* sur la même base.

R Фильм на обратимой пленке

S Película de inversión

REVIEW *See* APPRAISAL

RIGHT OF ACCESS *See* ACCESS

RIGHT OF PRIVACY *See* PRIVACY

ROLL

(1) A *document* or assembly of *documents* consisting of one or more *membranes* of *parchment* or *sheets (1)* of *paper* in which the *membranes* and/or *sheets (1)* are sewn together end to end and rolled. In UK, also used for *documents* placed in a pile, aligned at the head and then sewn and rolled, retaining the name even when not rolled.
(2) A *document* wound in cylindrical form for convenience of storage.
(3) A *document* listing the names of persons drawn up for a special purpose, e.g. nominal roll, muster roll, electoral roll, tax roll.
(4) A length of *microfilm,* usually 30 metres, on a carrier *reel.*

D (1) Rol, rotulus
   (2/3/4) Rol

G (1) Rotulus
   (2) Rolle
   (3) Liste, Matrikel, (gelegentlich auch:) Rolle (z.B. Stammrolle)
   (4) Rolle

I (1) Rotolo
  (2) Documento arrotolato
  (3) Ruolo, matricola, lista
  (4) Bobina

(1) ROLE (1)   421

Document formé par l'assemblage de deux ou de plusieurs *feuilles* de *parchemin* ou de *papier* cousues bout à bout et enroulées; le terme est aussi utilisé (U.K.) pour désigner des *documents* cousus par les côtés soit enroulés, soit pliés.
(2) ROULEAU (2)
Document enroulé en cylindre pour en faciliter le rangement.
(3) ROLE (2), MATRICULE
Liste nominative de personnes établie à des fins spécifiques.
(4) ROULEAU (3)
Longueur de *microfilm* enroulé sur *bobine*, généralement de 30 mètres.

R (1/2) Столбец, свиток
   (3) Список, реестр
   (4) Рулон микрофильма

S (1) Rollo
  (2) Documento enrollado
  (3) Lista, rollo
  (4) Rollo

ROTARY CAMERA

A *microfilm* camera so constructed that the *original document* and *film* are moved simultaneously by connected transport mechanisms avoiding relative movement between *film* and *document* during exposure. *See also* PLANETARY CAMERA: STEP-AND-REPEAT CAMERA.

D Rotatiecamera

G Durchlaufkamera

CAMÉRA CINÉTIQUE   422

Appareil de prise de *vues* pour *microfilm* construit de manière à faire avancer simultanément les *documents* et la surface sensible pendant la durée de l'exposition; naguère dite caméra dynamique. *Voir aussi* (358) CAMÉRA STATIQUE.

R Микрофильмирующий аппарат динамической съемки

(continued)

I Macchina de ripresa in continuo

S Cámara rotatoria

ROW

Two or more *bays* of *shelving* connected end to end along the same axis. Also called a run.

D Rij, begin- en volgrek

G Reihe

I Filia

ÉPI SIMPLE 423

Ensemble de *rayonnages* simple-face juxtaposés bout à bout dans l'axe des *tablettes*.

R Ряд стеллажей

S Estantería

RUN *See* ROW

SAMPLING

In *appraisal,* the selection by varying methods of *items* from a body of *records (1)* made in such a way that, taken together, the *items* selected are representative of the whole.

D Steekproefsgewijze selectie

G Repräsentative Auswahl

I Campionatura

ÉCHANTILLONNAGE 424

Choix opéré, au cours du *tri*, selon des critères variables, notamment numériques, alphabétiques, topo-graphiques ou qualitatifs, d'une certaine proportion de *documents* qui, seuls conservés, seront con-sidérés comme représentant l'ensemble dont ils sont issus.

R Отбор образцов документов для хранения

S Muestreo

SCHEDULED RECORDS *See* SCHEDULING

SCHEDULING

The process of determining and recording in a *records schedule* the appropriate *retention period* and ultimate *disposal* of recurring *series;* the *records (1)* thus provided for are also called scheduled *records.*

D [Samenstellen van een lijst van voor vernietiging vatbare en van te bewaren stukken]

[– – –] 425

Processus de détermination et d'inscription dans un *réglement de tri* de la durée appropriée de *conservation (1)* et du sort dévolu à des catégories documentaires; les *documents* ainsi visés sont dits documents 'réglementés'.

R Определение сроков хране-ния документов в учрежде-ниях, Составление переч-ней

S –

G [Erarbeitung und Festlegung
von Bewertungs- und Aussonde-
rungsrichtlinien]

I Cφmpilazione dei massimari
di scarto

SCREENING
The examination of *records (1)*/
archives (1) to determine the
presence of *documents* or *information* subject to *restricted access*.
Also called segregation.

D Screening

G [Überprüfung von Schriftgut
im Hinblick auf Benutzungs-
beschränkungen]

I Scrematura

[– – –]   426

Examen des *archives (1)* visant à
y déceler soit la présence de
documents dont l'*accès* serait
réservé, soit des informations susceptibles d'en restreindre l'*accès*.

R –

S Revisión

SEAL
(1) A die/matrix, usually of
metal, engraved in intaglio
with the device or design
used to produce by the
application of pressure a
seal (2). Dies may be of
one-sided design only or in
pairs producing dissimilar
designs simultaneously on
each *seal (2)*.
(2) A piece of wax, lead or
other material upon which an
impression in relief from a
seal (1) has been made,
attached to a *document* or
applied to the face thereof,
originally serving as a means
of *authentication;* also used
to close a *document*. *See
also* COUNTERSEAL.

D (1) Zegelstempel
(2) Zegel

G (1) Siegelstempel, Typar
(2) Siegel

I (1) Matrice, tipario
(2) Sigillo

(1) MATRICE DE SCEAU   427
Moule, le plus souvent de métal,
portant gravé en creux et à l'envers,
la marque distincte (image et généralement légende) d'une personne physique ou morale, destinée à produire
un *sceau (2)* par pression sur un
support momentanément mou.
(2) SCEAU
Empreinte en relief obtenue par la
pression d'une *matrice,* sur un *support*
de cire, de cire à cacheter ou de métal,
fixée par divers procédés au *document*
qu'elle accompagne et destinée à
l'origine à servir de moyen d'*authentification* de celui-ci, utilisée également
pour réserver la connaissance du
contenu du *document* à un seul
destinataire. *Voir aussi* (113) CONTRE-
SCEAU.

R (1) Матрица печати
(2) Печать

S (1) Matriz
(2) Sello

SEAL CASTING/MOULDING

The making of direct and exact *copies* of impressions of *seals (2)* by the use of wax, plaster, rubber or other materials.

D Zegelafgietsel (maken van een)

G Siegelabguß(fertigung)

I Calco di sigilli

MOULAGE DE SCEAU 428

(1) Opération destinée à obtenir la *reproduction* d'un *sceau (2)* en coulant une matière solidifiable soit directement sur celui-ci, soit sur son empreinte — le creux — faite de matière exactement moulante.
(2) La *reproduction* ainsi obtenue.

R Муляж печати

S Moldear

SEARCH ROOM

A room or area in a *records centre/ archives (3)* where *documents* are consulted by *users* under the supervision of and with the assistance of archival personnel. Also called reading room or research room. *See also* INVENTORY ROOM.

D Studiezaal

G Benutzersaal

I Sala di studio (per gli studiosi); sala di lettura (per le ricerche uso giuridico)

SALLE DE LECTURE 429

Local d'un service d'*archives (2)* réservé à la consultation de *documents* sous la surveillance et avec l'aide du personnel d'archives. Dit aussi salle du public ou salle de consultation. *Voir aussi* (249) SALLE DES INVENTAIRES.

R Читальный зал архива

S Sala de lectura; sala de consulta

SEARCHER *See* USER

SECURITY CLASSIFICATION

The *restriction* on *access* to and use of *records (1)/archives (1)* or *information* therein imposed by a government in the interests of national security. The *records (1)* or *information* concerned are referred to as classified records or classified information.

D Rubricering

G (Verschlußsachen-)Einstufung

I Classificazione di segretezza

[– – –] 430

Restriction à la *communication* de *documents* imposée par un État pour raison de sécurité nationale.

R Засекречивание документов

S Restricción legal

SECURITY COPY

A *copy* of a *document* made in order to preserve the *information* it contains in case the *original* is lost or damaged. *See also* SECURITY MICROFILMING: VITAL RECORDS MANAGEMENT.

D Schaduwkopie

G Sicherungskopie

I Copia di sicurezza

COPIE DE SÉCURITÉ   431

Copie d'un *document* faite pour conserver l'information contenue dans l'*original,* pour le cas où celui-ci serait perdu ou détérioré. *Voir aussi* (433) MICROFILMAGE DE SÉCURITÉ.

R Страховая копия документа, микрофильм страхового фонда

S Copia de seguridad

SECURITY FONDS

A *collection* of *security copies* (USSR).

D Schaduwarchief

G [Bestand von Sicherungs-kopien]

I Collezione di copie di sicurezza

[– – –]   432

Collection de *copies de sécurité,* (URSS).

R Страховой фонд документов

S Fondo de seguridad

SECURITY MICROFILMING

The use of *microfilm* to provide *security copies. See also* PRESERVATION MICROFILMING: SECURITY FONDS: VITAL RECORDS MANAGEMENT.

D Schaduwverfilming

G Sicherungsverfilmung

I Microfilmatura di sicurezza

MICROFILMAGE DE SÉCURITÉ   433

Microfilmage effectué pour conserver, sous faibles dimensions, *copie* photographique de *documents* importants, pour le cas où les *originaux* viendraient à disparaître; le *microfilm* de sécurité est conservé dans un autre *magasin* d'archives que l'*original. Voir aussi* (431) COPIE DE SÉCURITÉ.

R Микрофильмирование в целях создания страхового фонда документов

S Microfilmación de seguridad

SEGREGATION *See* SCREENING

SELECTION *See* APPRAISAL

SELECTIVE RETENTION *See* APPRAISAL

SEMI-CURRENT RECORDS

Records (1) required so infrequent-
ly in the conduct of current business
that they should be transferred
from offices to a *records centre*
pending their ultimate *disposal*.
See also CURRENT RECORDS:
NON-CURRENT RECORDS.

D Semistatische archiefbescheiden

G Zurückgesetzte, ruhende
   Registratur

I Registratura di deposito,
   archivio di deposito

ARCHIVES INTERMÉDIAIRES   434

Ensemble de *documents* qui, tout
en ayant cessé d'être considérés
comme des *archives courantes*, ne
peuvent encore, en raison de leur
intérêt administratif, faire l'objet
de *tri* et d'*élimination*, et généralement conservés dans un *centre de
préarchivage. Voir aussi* (115)
ARCHIVES COURANTES.

R —

S Documentos semiactivos

SEMI-OFFICIAL RECORDS *See* OFFICE FILE(S) (2)

SERIES

Item or *documents* arranged in
accordance with a *filing plan/
system* or maintained as a unit
because they relate to a particular
function or subject, result from
the same activity, have a particular
form, or because of some other
relationship arising out of the
circumstances of their creation
or use. Also referred to as a record
series. *See also* CLASS.

D Serie

G Serie (vor allem bei Amts-
   büchern)

I Serie

[– – –]   435

Articles ou *documents* classés
ensemble et maintenus groupés
parce qu'ils se rapportent à une
fonction ou à un sujet donné, qu'ils
résultent d'une même activité,
revêtent une même forme, ou pour
tout autre raison indépendante de
leur création ou de leur utilisation;
appelés parfois série documentaire.

R —

S Serie

SERIES TITLE INVENTORY *See* INVENTORY

SHEET

(1) A rectangular piece of *paper*,
usually cut to a uniform size.
(2) A large piece of such *paper*
with a number of *pages* printed
on it, to be folded into a *signature (2)*

(1) FEUILLE DE PAPIER   436

Morceau de *papier* rectangulaire,
généralement de dimensions
normalisées.
(2) FEUILLE (1)
Surface de *papier* portant un certain

(continued)

for binding into a *volume*.
(3) An individual *map,* normally
one of a *series.*

D (1) Blad, vel
   (2) Vel
   (3) Blad

G (1/2) Bogen
   (3) (Karten)Blatt

I (1) Foglio
   (2) Foglio, folio
   (3) Foglio, tavola

SHELF

A thin, flat length of metal, wood,
or other material, usually one of
a set, built into a frame, or between two *uprights* or standards
which support it, for the storage
of *boxes* or *documents.*

D Plank, legbord

G (Regal)Brett

I Palchetto

SHELF LIST

A *list* of the *holdings* in a *records
centre/archives (3)* arranged in the
order of the contents of each *shelf.*
See also LOCATION INDEX/
REGISTER.

D Depotlijst

G Lagerungsübersicht

I Guida topografica

156

---

nombre de *pages* imprimées et qui,
pliée en *cahier,* forme l'un des éléments constitutifs d'un *volume.*

(3) FEUILLE (2)
Section d'une *carte* ou d'un *plan*
de grand format, découpée pour en
faciliter la consultation.

R (1) Лист бумаги
   (2) Печатный лист
   (3) Лист картографического
      документа

S (1) Hoja
   (2) Pliego
   (3) Mapa

TABLETTE   437

Plaque de tôle d'acier ou planche de
dimensions normalisées (en France,
1 m. de long et généralement 0,26 à
0,30 m. de large, pouvant supporter
une charge minimale de *documents*
de 100 kg), accrochée à deux *montants*
par l'intermédiaire de tasseaux ou par
des cornières amovibles permettant
son déplacement vertical, destinée au
rangement de *documents.*

R Полка стеллажа

S Balda, entrepaño, anaquel

INVENTAIRE TOPOGRAPHIQUE   438

Liste tenue à jour, indiquant, dans
l'ordre de la numérotation des
magasins, des étages, des *travées* et
des *tablettes,* la place exacte occupée
par les *fonds, collections* et *documents*
conservés dans un service d'*archives (2).*
Voir (438) REGISTRE TOPO-
GRAPHIQUE.

R Постеллажный топографи-
   ческий указатель

S Inventario topográfico

SHELVING

(1) Collectively, the *shelves* upon which *records (1)* / *archives (1)* are stored. Also called racking.
(2) The process of placing *records (1)/archives (1)* on *shelves* in the course of *arrangement (2)*.

D (1) Planklengte
(2) Plaatsing, berging

G (1) Regalanlage
(2) Einlagerung

I (1) Scaffalatura
(2) Disposizione dei documenti sulla scaffalatura

SHOWCASE *See* DISPLAY CASE

SHREDDING

The *destruction* of *documents* by mechanical cutting.

D Versnipperen

G Aktenvernichtung mit dem Reißwolf

I Trinciatura

SIGILLOGRAPHY

The science dealing with *seals*.

D Zegelkunde, sigillografie

G Siegelkunde, Sphragistik

I Sfragistica, sigillografia

SIGNATURE

(1) The name of a person written in his own hand. Also known as an *autograph*.
(2) A large *sheet* which, when folded to *page* size, forms one section of a *volume*. Also called quire.
(3) A number, letter or word at the bottom of the first *page* in *signature (2)* showing in what

RAYONNAGE 439

(1) Ensemble de *tablettes* destinées au rangement des documents d'*archives (1)*.
(2) [Opération de mise en place des *archives (1)* sur les *tablettes* d'un *magasin*.]

R (1) Стеллажное оборудование
(2) Размещение документов на полках стеллажей

S (1) Estantería
(2) Estantear

DÉCHIQUETAGE 440

Procédé de destruction des *documents* par découpage automatique en minces lanières.

R Измельчение документов, выделенных к уничтожению

S Trituración

SIGILLOGRAPHIE 441

Science appliquée à l'étude des *sceaux*.

R Сигиллография

S Sigilografía

(1) SIGNATURE (1) 442

Nom qu'une personne appose de sa propre main sur un *document* pour indiquer qu'elle en est l'auteur ou qu'elle en avalise la teneur.
(2) CAHIER
Elément d'un *volume* formé par une *feuille (1)* de *papier* pliée en *pages* au format de celui-ci.
(3) SIGNATURE (2)
Nombre, lettre ou mot figurant au

(continued)

order that section is to be
gathered for *binding*.

D (1) Handtekening
   (2) Katern
   (3) Signatuur

G (1) Unterschrift
   (2) Lage
   (3) Lagenbezeichnung

I (1) Firma, sottoscrizione
     autografo
   (2) Quaterno, quinterno
   (3) Segnatura, richiamo

bas de la première *page* d'un *cahier*,
indiquant la place que cette unité
doit occuper dans un *volume* lors de
l'assemblage.

R (1) Подпись, автограф
   (3) Сигнатура

S (1) Firma
   (2) Cuadernillo
   (3) Signatura

SILKING

A process used in *restoration* of
a *document* by pasting silk gauze,
or a substitute tissue to each
side of a *sheet (1)*.

D Cacheren

G Einbettung mit Seidengaze

I Rinforzo con velo di seta,
velatura in seta

SÉRICOLLAGE 443

Procédé de *restauration* d'un
feuillet par collage de mousseline de
soie ou autre tissu similaire sur
chacune de ses faces.

R Реставрация документов
  с помощью шелковки

S —

SILVER HALIDE FILM

A type of *film* using silver-halide
sensitized materials for the
production of latent *images*.

D Zilverhalidefilm

G Silber-Halogen-Film

I Film agli alogenuri de
argento

FILM ARGENTIQUE 444

Type de *film* obtenu grâce à
l'action de la lumière sur les halo-
génures d'argent et permettant de
bonnes et durables *reproductions*.

R Галоидно-серебряная
  пленка

S Película de sales de plata

SIZING

A process used in *restoration* to
reinforce a *document* by applying
a paste, glaze or filler by immersion,
spray or brush.

ENCOLLAGE 445

Procédé de *restauration* destiné à
renforcer un *document* par application
d'une pâte, d'un vernis ou d'une
matière obturante par immersion,
vaporisation ou brossage.

(continued)

D Lijmen

G Nachleimen, Angießen

I Ricollatura

R **Импрегнирование**

S Consolidación

SKIPPET
A small box, usually of wood or metal, used to protect a *seal (2)* attached to a *document*. Also used for boxes protecting both *document* and *seal(s) (2)*.

D (Zegel)doos

G (Siegel)Kapsel

I Teca

ÉTUI À SCEAU · 446
Petite boîte de bois ou de métal servant à protéger le *sceau (2)* appendu à un *document;* parfois boîte protégeant à la fois le *document* et son ou ses *sceaux (2)*.

R [**Футляр для хранения вислой печати**]

S Cazoleta, estuche

SLIDE
A single *positive* on transparent material held in a mount and intended for projection. *See also* TRANSPARENCY.

D Dia

G Dia(positiv)

I Diapositiva

DIAPOSITIVE · 447
Vue positive sur matériau transparent montée dans un cadre et destinée à la projection.

R **Слайд**

S Diapositiva, transparencia

SMOKE DETECTOR *See* FIRE DETECTION SYSTEM

SOFTWARE
A set of *computer programs,* procedures and associated *documentation (2)* concerned with the operation of an *automatic data processing* system as distinct from *hardware*.

D Programmatuur, software

G Software

I Software

LOGICIEL · 448
Ensemble de *programmes* et de procédés, parfois avec la *documentation (2)* qui leur est associée, relatifs au fonctionnement d'un *ordinateur;* s'oppose à *matériel*.

R **Программное обеспечение ЭВМ**

S Logical, logicial

SOLANDER CASE *See* DOCUMENT CASE

SOLVENT LAMINATION *See* HAND LAMINATION

SOUND RECORDING
  A *disc, tape,* filament or other
  medium on which sound has been
  recorded. Also called phonogram.

D Geluidsopname

G Tonaufzeichnung

I Registrazione sonora

ENREGISTREMENT SONORE   449
  (1) Fixation de sons (paroles, chant,
  musique, bruits) sur un *support*
  approprié grâce à un appareillage
  spécialisé. Dit aussi phonogramme.
  (2) Résultat de ce travail, tel que
  disque, ruban.

R Звукозапись,
   Фонодокумент

S Cinta sonora, disco sonora

SOUND TAPE *See* PHONOTAPE

SOURCE DATA AUTOMATION
MANAGEMENT
  The application of *records
  management* principles and
  techniques to the use of
  automatic data processing
  in the recording of *data (1)*
  primarily in machine-readable
  form rather than in *hard
  copy* (US).

D —

G Daten-Organisation

I —

[— — —]   450
  Application des principes de la
  gestion des documents aux procédés automatiques utilisés pour
  l'enregistrement des *données*
  existant primitivement sous forme
  lisible en machine plutôt que sous
  forme informatique.

R Организация машиночитае-
   мых документов

S —

SPACE-SAVING MICROFILMING *See* DISPOSAL MICROFILMING

SPECIAL LIST
  A category of *finding aid* that
  uses as the unit of *entry (3),
  series, file unit* or *document,* to
  call attention to these particular
  items within a *record group,* to
  bring together *information* on all
  such *items* in several *record
  groups* relating to particular

[— — —]   451
  Type d'*instrument de recherches* qui
  prend comme unité d'entrée la 'series'
  au sens US, le *dossier* ou le *document*
  pour attirer l'attention sur ces *articles*
  à l'intérieur d'une *série d'archives,* pour
  rassembler les informations relatives à
  tous les *articles* similaires se trouvant
  dans plusieurs 'series' traitant du même

topic, or to expand the discriptive detail provided in *series entries* in *inventories* (US).

D –

G Repertorium

I Reportorio, guida tematica, inventario analitica

sujet, ou pour développer les *analyses* fournies dans les *inventaires* sous forme d'entrées de 'series' (US.)

R –

S Repertorio

SPLICING

The joining together of two segments of *roll film*.

D Montage

G Klebeverbindung (von Filmstreifen)

I ι Giunzione

COLLURE 452

Collage par les bords de deux segments d'un *rouleau* de *microfilm*.

R **Склейка**

S Empalmar

SPRINKLER SYSTEM

A *fire extinguishing system* utilizing water carried in overhead pipes to a series of sprinkler heads, individually and automatically activated by mechanical or electronic means. *See also* FIRE DETECTION SYSTEM.

D Sprinklerinstallatie

G Sprinkler-Anlage

I Sistema di estinzione automatica a pioggia

SPRINKLER 453

Système d'extinction automatique *d'incendie* utilisant des têtes d'arrosage à commande mécanique ou électronique, alimentées par des canalisations fixées au plafond. *Voir* (189) SYSTÈME D'EXTINCTION D'INCENDIE.

R **Спринклерная система автоматической пожарной защиты**

S Rociador

STACK/STORAGE PLAN

A plan of a stack or storage area indicating placement of *shelving* or other storage equipment and actual or intended use of the available space.

D [Stellingenplan]

G Lagerungsplan

I Piano di installazione della scaffalatura

[Plan de gestion de l'espace] 454

Plan des *magasins* indiquant l'emplacement des rayonnages et autres éléments de stockage et l'utilisation actuelle ou future de l'espace disponible.

R **План архивохранилища**

S Plan de instalación

STACKS
The storage areas in a *records centre/archives (3)*. Also called strongrooms.

D Depot(s)

G Magazin(e)

I Depositi, magazzini

MAGASIN 455
Ensemble des aires destinées à la conservation matérielle des *documents* dans un service d'*archives (2)*.

R Архивохранилище

S Depósito

STAFF FILE *See* PERSONNEL FILE

STAMPED PAPER
Paper bearing an applied or embossed government revenue stamp upon it.

D Gezegeld papier

G Stempelpapier

I Carta bollata

PAPIER TIMBRÉ 456
Papier portant un timbre fiscal collé ou frappé.

R Гербовая бумага

S Papel timbrado

STAMPING
The placing of an identifying stamp upon a *document* or the *leaves* thereof denoting that it is the property of or in the legal *custody* of *archives (2)*, within which the individual *reference number* may also be placed. Also called marking. *See also* NUMBERING.

D Stempelen

G Stempeln

I Timbratura

ESTAMPILLAGE 457
Application, à des fins de contrôle et de sécurité, sur un *document*, – éventuellement sur chacun de ses *feuillets* –, à l'aide d'un cachet identifiant son propriétaire ou détenteur public ou privé, d'une marque à l'encre indélébile.

R Штемпелевание архивных документов

S Sellado

STANDARDIZED FILING PLAN/SYSTEM
A *filing plan/system* prescribed for all agencies of a particular type or for all units of a particular agency, institution or organisation or for certain types of *records (1)* common to several agencies.

[Cadre de classement normalisé] 458
Cadre de classement prescrit soit à toutes les administrations d'un type donné, soit à tous les services d'une administration, soit pour le *traitement* de certains types de *documents* communs à plusieurs administrations.

(continued)

D Ordeningsplan

G Einheitsaktenplan

I Titolario unificato

R Примерная номенклатура дел

S —

STATE ARCHIVAL FONDS

The totality of *documents* of political, scientific, economic, social or cultural significance belonging to the state and subject to central registration and *preservation* in the *archives (2)/(3)* of the state (USSR).

D —

G (DDR:) Staatlicher Archiv-fonds

I Patrimonio archivistico statale

[Fonds des archives d'État] **459**

Totalité des *documents* de caractère politique, scientifique, économique, social ou culturel appartenant à l'État, sujets à un enregistrement central et devant être conservés dans les *archives (2)* de l'État (URSS).

R Государственный архивный фонд

S Fondos de archivos estatales

STATE ARCHIVES *See* CENTRAL ARCHIVES

STEP-AND-REPEAT CAMERA

A camera used to produce *micro-fiche*. *See also* PLANETARY CAMERA: ROTARY CAMERA.

D Microfichecamera

G Mikrofiche-Kamera

I Macchina da ripresa per microschede

CAMÉRA POUR MICROFICHES **460**

Caméra utilisée pour la production de *microfiches*.

R Микрофильмирующий аппарат для производства микро-фиш

S Cámara de microfichas

STEREOGRAPHICS

Pairs of *photographs* taken from different angles which, when viewed through a stereoscope, are seen as a single picture apparently having depth or three dimensions.

D Stereofoto(s)

G Stereo(skop)bilder

I Fotografie stereoscopiche

STÉRÉOGRAMMES **461**

Ensemble de deux *photographies* d'un même objet, jumelées, prises par deux objectifs parallèles, et qui, vues à travers un stéréoscope, donnent l'impression du relief.

R Стереоскопия

S Estereografías

STILL PICTURE *See* PHOTOGRAPH

STOCKTAKING

The checking of the *holdings* of *archives (3)* to ensure that all *items* are either in place or otherwise accounted for.

D Bestandsopname

G (Bestands)Revision

I Revisione dei fondi

RÉCOLEMENT   462

(1) Vérification et pointage de l'ensemble ou de partie du contenu d'un *dépôt* d'*archives (3)* pour s'assurer que chaque *article* se trouve en place ou est représenté par un *fantôme*.
(2) *Document* consignant le détail de cette vérification.

R Проверка наличия дел

S Recuento

STORAGE *See* MEMORY

STRIPPING *See* WEEDING

STRONGROOM *See* STACK

SUB-GROUP

A body of *records (1)* /*archives (1)* within an *archive group, fonds* or *record group*, usually those of a subordinate administrative unit. Also referred to as records sub-group.

A Afdeling

G Teilbestand, Unterabteilung eines Bestandes

I Fondo, archivio, registratura

[Fonds secondaire]   463

Ensemble d'*archives (2)* appartenant à un *fonds*, généralement constitué par les *archives (1)* d'une unité administrative subordonnée.

R Подгруппа документов внутри архивного фонда

S Sub-serie

SUBJECT ARRANGEMENT *See* ARRANGEMENT

SUBJECT FILE

A *file (1)* in which the *documents* relate to a specific subject matter, frequently based upon a *filing plan/system*. *See also* CASE PAPERS/FILES.

DOSSIER PAR SUJET   464

Dossier groupant des *documents* relatifs à un sujet donné.

D Onderwerpsdossier
G Betreffakte, Sachakte
I Fascicolo, pratica

R Дело, сформированное по предметному признаку

S Expediente por materias

SUBJECT GUIDE *See* GUIDE (2)

SUB-SERIES
  Items or *documents* within a
  series readily separable in terms
  of filing arrangement, physical
  class, type, form or content.

[– – –]   465
  Articles ou *documents* qui, à
  l'intérieur d'une *série (3)* sont
  aisément identifiables en termes
  de *classement*, de catégorie
  physique, de type, de forme ou de
  contenu.

D Rubriek
G –
I Sottoserie

R –
S Sub-serie

SUBSTITUTION MICROFILMING *See* DISPOSAL MICROFILMING

SUMMARY GUIDE *See* SUMMARY OF RECORDS

SUMMARY INVENTORY *See* INVENTORY

SUMMARY OF RECORDS
  A *list* enumerating the *holdings*
  of *archives (2)* by *archive groups*
  and *classes* therein giving only
  title of the *group* and *class,* and
  usually date range and quantity.
  Also called list of *holdings* or
  summary guide. *See also* GUIDE.

ÉTAT SOMMAIRE OU ÉTAT DES   466
FONDS
  Instrument de recherche décrivant
  de façon sommaire tout ou partie du
  contenu d'un *dépôt* d'*archives (2)*
  par *fonds* et divisions de *fonds*, en
  fournissant seulement pour chacun
  d'eux, l'intitulé, les dates extrêmes,
  le nombre d'*articles* et le *métrage
  linéaire.*

D [Bestandslijst]
G Beständeliste
I Guida, guida-inventorio

R Список фондов архива
S Inventario general

SURVEY

(1) A *document* assembling *information* relating to specified subject(s) or problem(s) as a basis for planning and decision-making.
(2) A *document* resulting from the formal inspection of landed property giving details of its nature, extent, location, sometimes used as the basis for tax assessment.

D (1) Enquete
   (2) Legger

G (1) Bestandsaufnahme
   (2) Kataster

I (1) Scheda di rilevazione
  (2) Catasto

(1) ENQUÊTE PRÉLIMINAIRE 467

Document réunissant des informations sur un sujet ou un problème donné et destiné à servir de base à une planification et / ou à une prise de décision.

(2) ENQUÊTE CADASTRALE

Document résultant d'une inspection administrative des propriétés foncières et fournissant des précisions sur leur emplacement, leur nature ou leur étendue, servant parfois de base à l'assiette d'impôts.

R (1) Информационный обзор
   (2) Земельный кадастр

S (1) Encuesta
   (2) Catastro

TAPE-RECORDING *See* SOUND RECORDING

TARGET

A *document* containing *information,* coding, or resolution test patterns, used in microfilming.

D Testbeeld

G Vorspann

I Lavagna, scheda tecnica

MIRE 468

Ensemble des informations techniques et autres données utiles fournies au *lecteur* en tête d'un *microfilm.*

R Тест—объект для микрофильмов

S Cartela

TECHNICAL DRAWING

A *plan,* elevation, cross-section, detail, diagram or *map* made for use in an engineering, architectural or other technical context.

D Technische tekening

G Technische Zeichnung

I Disegno tecnico

DESSIN TECHNIQUE 469

Dessin à échelle réduite, généralement sous forme de *plan*, coupe, élévation, ou de diagramme, utilisé en architecture, ingéniérie ou autre contexte technique. *Voir aussi* (356) PLAN.

R Технические рисунки

S Dibujo técnico

TERMINAL
A *peripheral* in a *computer* or
communication system by which
data (1) are entered or retrieved.

D Station, terminal

G Terminal

I Terminale

Périphérique ou ensemble de
périphériques d'*entrée – sortie*
capable d'échanger des *données (1)*
avec une *unité centrale* par
télécommunications.

R Терминал

S Terminal

TERRITORIAL PROVENANCE
The concept, deriving from the
principle of provenance, that
records (1)/archives (1) should
be preserved in or restored to the
archives (2) having *archival
jurisdiction* within the territory
in which they were accumulated,
excluding *documents* arising
from diplomatic representation
and military operations. *See also*
TERRITORIALITY/TERRITORIAL
PERTINENCE.

D [Territoriale herkomstbeginsel]

G Standortprinzip

I Provenienza territoriale

Concept dérivé du *principe du respect
des fonds* selon lequel les *archives (1)*
devraient être conservées dans les
services d'*archives (2)* ayant juridiction
sur le territoire dans lequel elles ont été
produites, à l'exclusion des *documents*
élaborés par des représentations diplomatiques ou résultant d'opérations mili-
taires.

R Принцип территориальной
принадлежности

S Procedencia territorial

TERRITORIALITY/
TERRITORIAL PERTINENCE
The concept, as opposed to the
principle of provenance, that
records (1)/archives (1) created
in a place outside the territory
with whose affairs they deal
should be transferred to the
custody of the *archives (2)*
having *archival jurisdiction*
within the territory to which
the substantive content of the
records (1)/archives (1) relate.
See also TERRITORIAL
PROVENANCE.

Concept opposé au *principe du
respect des fonds* selon lequel, sans
tenir compte de leur lieu de création,
les *archives (1)* devraient être
remises au service d'*archives (2)*
ayant juridiction archivistique sur
le territoire auquel se rapporte
leur contenu.

(continued)

D [Territoriale pertinentie-
beginsel]

G Territoriale Pertinenz

I Térritorialità, pertinanza
territoriale

R [Классификация и размещение
документов по принципу
территориальной принадлеж-
ности]

S Pertinencia territorial

TEXTUAL RECORDS/ARCHIVES
A term used to distinguish
records (1)/archives (1) in
manuscript or *typescript* from
audio-visual, cartographic and
*machine-readable records/
archives.*

D [Conventionele archief-
bescheiden]

G —

I Documenti/archivi scritti

ARCHIVES TEXTUELLES 473
Terme désignant les *archives (1)*
manuscrites, dactylographiées,
multigraphiées ou imprimées,
par opposition aur *archives audio-
visuelles,* mécanographiques ou
informatiques, dites 'archives
non textuelles'.

R Текстовой документ

S —

THERMOGRAPHY
Photocopying processes relying
upon heat for formation of the
image.

D [Warmtekopieren]

G Wärmekopierverfahren

I Termografia

THERMOGRAPHIE 474
Procédé de *photocopie* utilisant la
chaleur pour obtenir la formation
de l'*image.*

R Термография

S Termografía

THERMOPLASTIC LAMINATION
A mechanically assisted process,
generally preceded by *deacidification* of reinforcing damaged or
deteriorated *paper documents* by
enclosing them between two *sheets*
of plastic foil, usually cellulose
acetate, and two *sheets* of tissue
if not already incorporated in the
foil, which, through the application
of heat and pressure, become
thermoplastic and impregnate the
original. See also HAND LAMI-
NATION.

LAMINATION THERMOPLASTIQUE 475
Procédé assisté mécaniquement,
destiné à renforcer, généralement
après *désacidification,* les *documents*
sur *papier* détériorés en les enserrant
entre deux *feuilles* de matériau
plastique, généralement d'acétate
de cellulose, et de deux *feuilles (1)*
de *papier* pur chiffon, lequel peut
avoir été incorporé au préalable au
matériau plastique ; sous l'action
conjointe de la chaleur et de la
pression, ce matériau devient thermoplastique et adhère à l'*original.*
Voir aussi (218) LAMINATION
MANUELLE.

(continued)

D [Thermoplastisch lamineren]

G Heißlaminierung

I Laminazione termoplastica, laminazione a caldo

R Импрегнирование. Ламинирование

S Laminación

THESAURUS

A controlled vocabulary of semantically related terms which covers one or more specific fields of knowledge. *See also* INDEX: KEYWORD.

D Thesaurus

G Thesaurus

I Thesaurus

THESAURUS 476

Vocabulaire généralement spécialisé, cohérent et limité de mots, assortis de leurs correspondances sémantiques, choisis de manière à pouvoir représenter toutes les notions figurant dans un texte donné et ainsi servir en *informatique* à l'établissement d'*index*. *Voir* (235) INDEX, (253) NOM DE MATIÈRE.

R Тезаурус

S Thesaurus

TIPPING-IN

The insertion of a single *leaf* or *sheet (1)* into a *volume* by pasting a narrow margin at the binding edge. *See also* GUARD.

D (Lijmen) inlijmen

G Einkleben

I Imbrachettatura

MONTAGE SUR ONGLET 477

Insertion d'un ou plusieurs *feuillets* dans un *volume* par collage d'une étroite bande au fond du *cahier*.

R [Вклейка листов при переплете]

S Poner guardas

TITLE DEED(S) *See* DEED

TOPONYMY *See* ONOMASTICS

TOTAL ARCHIVES

Archives (2) whose responsibilities cover *records (1)/archives (1)* and other materials of research value irrespective of *provenance (1)* or type of *document* (Canada).

[— — —] 478

Archives (2) dont la responsabilité couvre *fonds* et *collections* et autres matériaux de recherche, sans égard pour la *provenance (1)* ou le type de *document* (Canada anglophone).

(continued)

D –   R –
G –   S –
I –

TRANSACTIONAL FILES *See* CASE PAPERS/FILES

TRANSACTIONS *See* PROCEEDINGS

TRANSCRIPT
(1) A *copy* or *reproduction* in so
far as the resources of script
and/or typography allow of an
original document, with the
exception that *abbreviations,*
if their interpretation is clear,
may be extended.
(2) In legal proceedings, an
exact *copy* of a text.
(3) A verbatim written, typed or
printed version of the spoken
word, e.g. proceedings in a
court of law, an *oral history*
interview.

D (1) Transcriptie
   (2) Authentiek afschrift
   (3)   –

G (1) Transkription
   (2) Wortgetreue Abschrift
   (3) Transkription

I (1) Trascrizione
   (2) Copia autentica
   (3) Verbalizzazione letterale

TRANSCRIPTION 479
(1) *Copie* d'un *document original,*
ou de sa *reproduction* dans la mesure
où les ressources de l'écriture ou de
la typographie le permettent, dans
laquelle les *abréviations* peuvent être
développées si leur interprétation est
sûre.
(2) [Dans le procédures juridiques,
copie exacte d'un texte.]
(3) Mise par écrit, mot à mot, sous
forme dactylographiée ou imprimée,
d'un texte parlé, comme les *procès-
verbaux* d'une cour de justice ou un
entretien d'*histoire orale.*

R (1) Передача текста доку-
     мента
   (2) Точная копия текста
   (3) Транскрипция

S (1) Transcripción
   (2) Copia literal, copia translado
   (3) Transcripción

TRANSFER
(1) The act involved in a change
of physical *custody* of *records
(1)/archives (1)* with or without
change of legal title.
(2) *Records(1)/archives (1)* so
transferred.

1. VERSEMENT (1) 480
Opération par laquelle la *conservation*
d'*archives (1)* passe de l'administration d'origine à un *centre de préarchivage* ou à un service d'*archives (2),* ou
bien d'un *centre de préarchivage* à un
service d'*archives (2),* avec ou sans
changement de propriété.

(continued)

2. VERSEMENT (2)
Ensemble des *documents* ainsi
transférés.
3. ARCHIVAGE
Envoi d'*archives (1)* n'ayant plus
d'utilité courante dans un local ou un
service spécialisé aux fins de *conservation.* (Le verbe correspondant est
'archiver').

D (1) Overbrenging, overdracht
(2) Overdracht

G (1) Abgabe, Übergabe, Ablieferung
(2) Abgabe, Ablieferung

I (1) Trasferimento
(2) Versamento

R (1) Передача документов
на хранение
(2) Документы, переданные
на хранение

S (1) Transferencia
(2) Fondos transferidos

TRANSFER LIST
A list of *records (1)/archives (1)*
affected by a single *transfer (1).*

D Overdrachtslijst

G Abgabe-/Ablieferungsverzeich-
nis

I Elenco di versamento

BORDEREAU DE VERSEMENT 481
Liste donnant l'intitulé et les dates
extrêmes des *articles* faisant l'objet
d'un *versement (1).*

R Опись документов,
передаваемых на хранение

S Relación de transferencia

TRANSFER SCHEDULE *See* RECORDS SCHEDULE

TRANSPARENCY
A *negative* or *positive* on transparent material used for copying,
viewing or projecting by trans-
mitted light. *See also* SLIDE.

D Transparant

G Transparentkopie

I Trasparente

[– – –] 482
Copie positive ou *négative,* isolée
ou en bande, sur *support* transparent, destinée au tirage de *copies,*
à la vision ou à la projection.

R Диапозитив

S Transparencia

TREATMENT OF CORRESPONDENCE *See* CORRESPONDENCE MANAGEMENT

TYPESCRIPT
A typed *document*. See also
MANUSCRIPT.

D Getypt document

G Maschinenschrift(liches
Dokument)

I Dattiloscritto

DACTYLOGRAMME 483
Document tapé à la machine.

R Машинопись

S Documento mecanografiado

ULTRAFICHE
A *microfiche* with a *reduction
ratio* greater than 90X.

D Ultrafiche

G Ultrafiche

I –

ULTRAFICHE 484
Microfiche dont le taux de
réduction est égal ou supérieur
à 1/90.

R [микрофиша с ультрамикро-
изображениями]

S Ultraficha

ULTRA-VIOLET LAMP
A lamp emitting ultra-violet
radiation for the examination
of faded *documents*. Also called
quartz lamp and Wood's lamp.

D Kwartslamp

G Quarzlampe

I Lampada di Wood, lampada
a raggi ultravioletti,
lampada al quarzo.

LAMPE DE WOOD 485
Lampe émettrice de rayons ultra-
violets facilitant la lecture des
écritures pâlies; dite aussi lampe
à quartz.

R Ультрафиолетовая лампа.
Кварцевая лампа

S Lámpara de cuarzo/ultra-
violeta/Wood

UNITISED FILM
Roll microfilm separated into
individual *frames* or *strips* and
inserted into a *film jacket* or
carrier.

D –

G –

I Spezzone (di microfilm)

BANDE DE MICROFILM 486
Segment d'un rouleau de *microfilm* inséré dans une *jaquette*.

R Отрезок микрофильма в
джекете

S Tira de película

UPRIGHT
The *shelving* element which frames
the width of the *bay* and supports
the *shelves* within the *bay*.

MONTANT 487
Elément séparant deux *travées*
et supportant l'une des extrémités
des *tablettes* par l'intermédiaire de
tassaux ou de cornières.

(continued)

D Staander

G [Trägerelement einer Regalanlage]

I Montante

R Стойка стеллажа

S _Montante

USER

An individual who consults *records (1)/archives (1)*, usually in a *search room*. Also called reader, researcher, searcher.

D Gebruiker

G Benutzer

I Studioso, lettore, utente

CHERCHEUR · 488

Personne qui consulte des *archives (1)* généralement dans une *salle de lecture*. Dit aussi, à tort, lecteur.

R Исследователь, читатель

S Lector, investigador, usario

VACUUM DRYING

The treatment of water-soaked *documents* by placing them at room temperature in a vacuum chamber, slowly evacuating the air until the temperature reaches freezing point and then proceeding through a series of cycles, the number dependent on the wetness of the *documents,* in which the chamber is alternately filled with hot, dry air and evacuated until the temperature of the documents is raised to 50°F. *See also* FREEZE DRYING.

D Vacuumdrogen

G Vakuumtrocknung

I Essicatore con congelamento sotto vuoto

SÉCHAGE PAR LE VIDE 489

Traitement de *documents* imprégnés d'eau en les enfermant à la température d'environnement dans une chambre à vide, en évacuant l'air graduellement jusqu'à ce que la température atteigne le point de congélation, puis en introduisant et en évacuant, une ou plusieurs fois, de l'air chaud et sec jusqu'à ce que la température des documents atteigne 10°. *Voir aussi* (206) SÉCHAGE À FROID.

R Сушка документов в вакуумной камере

S Secado en cámara de vacio

VALUATION

The determination, based upon fair market prices, of the monetary value of *manuscripts* or *records (1)*.

ESTIMATION 490

Évaluation de la valeur marchande de *manuscrits* ou d'*archives (1)*.

(continued)

D Taxatie

G Wertfestsetzung

I Valutazione

R денежная оценка докумен-тов

S Valuación, tasación, evaluación

VAULT
A maximum security storage area constructed of fire-resistant material and structurally independent from the building in which it is located.

D Kluis

G Tresor(raum)

I –

CHAMBRE FORTE 491
Local réservé, dans un service d'*archives (2)*, à la *conservation* de *documents* précieux ou confidentiels, isolé dans le bâtiment où il se trouve, construit de manière à offrir le maximum de sécurité contre toute espèce de sinistre, et en principe inviolable par l'homme.

R Сейфовое архивохранилище, отсек – сейф

S Cámara de seguridad

VELLUM *See* PARCHMENT

VERTICAL FILING
The storage of *documents* in an upright position as distinguished from *flat-filing*.

D Verticale berging, staande berging

G Stehende Aufbewahrung

I Disposizione verticale dei documenti sulla scaffalatura

RANGEMENT VERTICAL 492
Mode de rangement où les *documents* reposent sur leur tranche inférieure; s'oppose au rangement à plat.

R Вертикальное хранение документов

S Instalación vertical

VESICULAR FILM
A type of *film* in which nitrogen released during exposure expands on subsequent heating to form minute vesicles (bubbles) which produce an *image* by light scattering.

FILM VÉSICULAIRE 493
Type de *film* dans lequel l'azote libéré pendant l'exposition se répand sous l'effet de la chaleur subséquente et forme des bulles minuscules qui produisent une *image* par diffusion de la lumière.

D Vesiculaire film
G Vesikularfilm
I Pellicola vesicolare

R Везикулярный фильм
S Película vesicular

VIDEO DISC/DISK

A flat circular *medium* upon
the surfaces of which *images* can
be recorded and stored.

D Beeldplaat
G Videoplatte
I Videodisco

VIDÉODISQUE 494

Support circulaire plat dont les
surfaces permettent l'enregistrement et la conservation d'*images*.

R Видеодиск
S Video-disco

VIDEOTAPE

A *magnetic tape* on which visual
images are electronically recorded,
with or without sound.

D Videoband
G Videoband
I Videonastro, videotape

BANDE VIDÉO 495

Bande magnétique sur laquelle
les *images* sont enregistrées électro-
niquement, avec ou sans *enregistrement sonore*.

R Видеограмма
S Video-cinto

VIDIMUS

A *charter* in which the grantor
states that an earlier *document*
has been seen and/or inspected,
which is now recited and confirmed.
Also called inspeximus (UK).

D Vidimus
G Vidimus
I Vidimus

VIDIMUS 496

Acte authentique par lequel une
autorité déclare avoir vu et con-
firme un texte antérieur qu'elle
transcrit en entier ou en partie;
dit aussi inspeximus (U.K.)

R Видимус
S Vidimus

VISUAL DISPLAY UNIT

A *peripheral* for visual presentation
of *data (1)* generated by a *computer,*
generally combined with a keyboard
or other device for entry of *data (1)*
and commands.

D Beeldschermeenheid
G Datensichtgerät
I Unità di visualizzazione

CONSOLE DE VISUALISATION 497

Périphérique destiné à la visualisation
de *données (1)* traitées par *ordinateur,*
en général couplées à un clavier ou à un
autre organe d'entrée de *données (1)*
ou d'instructions.

R Дисплей
S Pantalla

VITAL RECORDS MANAGEMENT
The application of *records management* principles and techniques to ensure the preservation of *records(1)* vital to the continuity of business in cases of emergency or after a disaster, frequently through the use of *security microfilming. See also* DISASTER PLAN.

D –

G [Behandlung von Schriftgut in Alarm- und Verteidigungs-fall]

I –

[– – –]   498
Application des principes et des techniques de la *gestion des documents* pour conserver, le plus souvent par un *microfilmage de sécurité,* la teneur des *documents* essentiels à la continuité du travail, en prévision d'une catastrophe.

R [Микрофильмирование доку-ментов особого практичес-кого значения]

S [Medidas de seguridad]

VITAL STATISTICS *See* CIVIL REGISTERS

VOLUME
Manuscript or printed *sheets* bound together within a cover.

D Deel, band

G Band

I Volume

VOLUME   499
Feuillets manuscrits, dactylographiés ou imprimés, brochés ou reliés sous couverture. Dit aussi *registre.*

R Том

S Volumen

VOUCHER
A *document* serving as evidence or proof, specifically, a receipt or statement attesting to the expenditure or receipt of money, usually accompanied by bills or other evidence of indebtedness or expenditure.

D Kasstuk

G (Rechnungs)Beleg

I Buono, mandato, documento giustificativo, pezza d'appoggio

PIECE JUSTIFICATIVE DE COMPTABILITÉ
Document probant et, précisément,   500
reçu ou déclaration attestant la sortie ou l'encaissement d'argent, en général accompagné de factures ou autres preuves d'endettement ou de dépense.

R Оправдательный документ

S Justificante

WASTE BOOK *See* DAYBOOK: JOURNAL

WATERMARK
A translucent mark in *paper* produced during manufacture.

D Watermerk

G Wasserzeichen, Papierzeichen

I Filigrana

FILIGRANE 501
Marque spécifique visible par transparence dans le *papier*, obtenue au cours de la fabrication.

R Водяной знак, Филигрань

S Filigrana

WEEDING
The removal of individual *documents* or *files (1)* lacking continuing value from a *series*. Also known as culling, purging or stripping.

D Uitschieten

G Ausdünnen

I Sfoltimento

[− − −] 502
Enlèvement d'*articles* destinés à l'*élimination*. *Voir* (22) TRI.

R −

S Expurgo

WINDOW REPAIR *See* FRAMING

WOOD'S LAMP *See* ULTRA-VIOLET LAMP

WORD *See* COMPUTER WORD

WORKING PAPERS
Documents, such as *drafts,* rough *notes,* and calculations, created or assembled and used in the analysis or preparation of other *documents.*

D [Voorbereidende stukken]

G Arbeitsunterlagen

I Documenti di lavoro, atti preparatori

DOCUMENTS PRÉPARATOIRES 503
Documents, tels que *brouillons, notes* informes, calculs établis ou réunis et exploités pour étudier ou élaborer d'autres *documents.*

R Рабочие документы

S Documentos de trabajo

WRIT *See* BRIEF (2)

XEROGRAPHY *See* ELECTROSTATIC PROCESS

Indices

Français
Nederlands
Deutsch
Italiano
Русский
Español

FRANÇAIS

L'ordre des termes est alphabétique. Figure entre crochets, la traduction, non usitée en français, des termes anglo-saxons.

Abréviations: B = Belgique
UK = Royaume uni
US = États-Unis d'Amérique

abréviation 1
[accès par dérogation] 89
accroissement 9
[accumulation] 8
acidité 349
acte 11
affiche 363
agrandissement 163
agrandisseur imprimant 164
aide-mémoire 95
aliénation 19
allée principale de circulation 18
analyse 166
aplatisseur 46
apostille 285
appareil de lecture 384
archivage 480
archives 33
archives administratives 129
archives audio-visuelles 36
archives cartographiques 60
archives centrales 68
archives cinématographiques 185 (1)
archives communales 271
archives courantes 115
archives cultuelles 81
archives de cabinet 212
archives de données informatiques 119
archives de familles 175
[archives de service regroupées 69]
archives déplacées 407
archives diplomatiques 138
archives économiques 54
archives générales 68
archives historiques 222
archives iconographiques 230
archives imprimées 370
archives informatiques 274
archives intermédiaires 434
archives littéraires 268
archives ministérielles 129, 307

archives nationales 68, 311
archives non textuelles 473
archives notariales 316
archives orales 327
archives photographiques 353
archives privées 373
archives publiques 381
archives régionales 401
archives textuelles 473
archiviste 34
archivistique 29 (1)
article 250 (1)
atelier de restauration 416
audiobande 350
authentication 71
authentification 37
autoclave 208
autographe 38 (1)

bande de microfilm 486
bande magnétique 276
bande perforée 382
bande sonore 350
bande vidéo 495
banque de données 120
base de données 121
bit 45
bobine 397 (1)
bordage 205
bordereau 267 (2)
bordereau d'élimination 267 (2)
bordereau d'envoi 267 (1)
bordereau de versement 481
bref 51 (1)
brouillon 153 (1)
bulle 52 (1, 2)
bulletin de demande 377
[bureau des archives courantes] 403

cadastre 176
cadre de classement 87

NEDERLANDS

189

DEUTSCH

194

ITALIANO

Русский

Аббревиатура 1

Автограф 38(1), 38(2), 225, 442(1)

Автоматизированная информационно-поисковая система 239

Автоматическая обработка данных 39

Авторское право 110

Административно-хозяйственные документы 227

Акт 11, 126

Акт о выделении документов к уничтожению 144

Актовая книга 402

[Альбом форм документов 202]

Апертурная карта 21

Аппарат контактного копирования 354(1)

Аппаратные средства в вычислительной машине 220

Археографическая деятельность 223

Архив 33(2), 69

Архив ведомства 69

Архив данных 119

Архив кинодокументов 185(2)

Архив литературы 268(2)

Архив министерства 307

Архив учреждения 129

Архивист 34

Архивная коллекция 93(1), 93(2), 283

Архивная опись 132, 248(1)

[Архивная опись, построенная по хронологии 79]

Архивная служба 33(2)

Архивное дело 29(2)

Архивное право 24

Архивные документы 28(2), 33(1)

Архивные фонды местных учреждений 27(1)

Архивные фонды нотариальных учреждений 316

Архивные фонды предприятий 54(1)

Архивный документ 146(1), 146(2), 250(2)

Архивный каталог 66

[Архивный каталог 211]

Архивный музей 31

Архивный справочник 187

Архивный фонд 28(1), 30, 33(1)

Архивный фонд деятелей или учреждений литературы 268(1)

Архивный фонд министерства 307

Архивный фонд учреждения 389

Архивный шифр 399

Архивоведение 29(1)

Архивохранилище 33(3), 455

Архивы предприятий 54(2)

Аудио-визуальные документы 36

Афиша 363

Аэрофотоснимок 16

База данных 121

Байт 55

Банк данных 120

Беловик 161, 162(2), 174

Бесхозные документы 169

[Бесшовное скрепление документов дела, книги при переплете 12]

Бит 45

Бланк документа 199(1)

Бобина 397(1), 397(2)

Бреве 51(1)

Булла 52(1), 52(2)

Бумага 337

212

213

ESPAÑOL

abreviatura 1
accesibilidad 2 (1)
acceso 2 (2)
acondicionamiento 35 (2)
acta 11, 308 (1), 374
acumulación 9
administración de archivos 29 (2)
adquisición 9
ampliación 163, 277
ampliadora 164
anaquel 437
anejo 50
aparator lector 384
aparato lector-impressor 385
archivística 29 (1)
archivador de planos 357
archivero 34
archivo 33 (2), 33 (3)
archivo activo 115
archivo administrativo 17
archivo central 69
archivo complementario (anejo) 20 (1)
archivo conjunto 251
archivo(s) desplazado(s) 407
archivo fotográfico 353
archivo general 68
archivo(s) histórico(s) 33 (1), 222
archivo de impresos 370 (1), 370 (2)
archivo intermedio 390
archivo literario 268 (1)
archivo(s) municipal(es) 271 (1)
archivo nacional 68, 311
archivo(s) notarial(es) 316
archivo oral 327
archivo regional 401
archivología 29 (1)
archivonomía 29 (1)
archivos administrativos 129
archivos cartográficos 60
archivos conjuntos 251
archivos diplomáticos 138
archivos eclesiásticos 81 (1)
archivos de empresa 54
archivos familiares 175
archivos iconográficos 230
archivos ministeriales 307
archivos privados 373
archivos públicos 381

asiento 166 (1)
atril 47
autenticación 37, 71 (1)
autógrafo 38 (1)
autorización de consulta 89

balda 437
banda magnética 276
banda sonora 350
banco de datos 120
base de datos 121
borrador 153 (1)
breve 51 (1)
bula (papal) 52 (1), 52 (2)

caja 48, 391
cámara estática 358
cámara de fumigación 208
cámara de microfichas 460
cámara procesadora 57
cámara rotatoria 422
cámara de seguridad 491
camisa 194
campo de imagen 204
carácter 72
carpeta 147, 360
carpetilla 194
carta 261 (1)
carta cerrada 263
carta de navegación 74
carta partida 77
carta(s) patente(s) 264
cartel 363
cartela 468
cartivana 216
cartucho 61
cartulario 62
carrete 397 (1)
catálogo 66
catastro 67, 176, 464 (2)
cazoleta 446 (1)
censal 408
censo 67
centro de proceso de datos 119
certificación 71 (1)
certificado 71 (2)
ciencia de la información 240
cifra 82 (1), 82 (2), 82 (3)
cinta perforadora 382
cinta sonora 449

justificante 500

laminación 475
laminación manual 218
laminación con seda 443
lámpara de cuarzo 485
lámpara ultravioleta 485
lámpara wood 485
lector 488
lector óptico 326
legado 42
legajo 53
legalización 71 (1)
letra(s) patente(s) 264
liberalización 125
liberar 152
libranza 153 (2)
libro de caja 64
libro de censos 408
libro copiador de cartas 262
[libro copiador de cartas] 265
libro mayor 258
libro de rentas 408
libros sacramentales 342
limpieza 88
liofilización 206
lista 421 (3)
lista de consultantes 236
lista de consultas 236
lista de expurgo/tría 194
logical 448
logicial 448

maceración 273
mandato 51 (2)
manuscrito 279
manuscritos literarios 269
mapa 284, 436
marco 204
material o equipo informático 220
matriz 286, 427 (1)
medidas de seguridad 498
„memorandum" 95
memoria 291
memorial 290 (2)
metro cúbico 114
metrología 293
metros lineales 266
microcopia 296
microficha 297

microficha opaca 294
microfilmación administrativa 13
microfilmación de seguridad 433
microfilmación de sustitución 145
microfilme 298
microfilme de complemento 10
microfilme de consulta 398
microfilme negativo 313
microfilme positivo 362
microfilme de preservación 365
microforma 302
micrografía 303
microimagen 304
microordenador 295, 305
miniordenador 306
minuta 153 (1), 308 (2)
modelo 199 (1), 199 (2)
moldear 428
momio 155
montante 487
moteado 203
muestreo 424

negativo 287, 312
neutralización 123
normalización de modelos 201
nota 317 (1), 317 (2), 317 (3)
nota interior 290 (1)
nota marginal 285
notación binaria 43
notas dorsales 160
numismática 319

octeto 55
ológrafo 225
onomástica 322
orden 51 (2)
orden de pago 153 (2)
ordenador 98
ordenanza(s) 328
organización de fondos de archivos 181
original 161, 162 (2), 329

página 333
paginación 334 (1), 334 (2)
palabra clave 253
paleografía 335
palimpsesto 336
pantalla 497
papel 337

saur

World Guide to Libraries
Internationales Bibliotheks-Handbuch

6th edition
Edited by Helga Lengenfelder
1983. XLVIII, 1186 pages. Bound.
DM 380.00. ISBN 3-598-20523-6
(Handbook of International Documentation and Information, Vol. 8)

The revised edition of this important directory lists over 43,000 libraries in 170 countries. Included are national, federal, and regional libraries, university and other academic libraries, and school and public libraries with holdings over 30,000 volumes, as well as special, government and parliamentary, religious, and business libraries with a minimum of 3,000 volumes. Included in each entry are complete address, telephone and telex numbers, cable address, year of founding, name of director, departments of major research libraries, information on important holdings and special collections, statistics on holdings, notes on loan policy, online services, and memberships in professional associations. The directory is arranged by continent and country, and within each country by type of library. A new alphabetical index of libraries completes the work.

World Guide to Special Libraries
Internationales Handbuch
der Spezialbibliotheken

Edited by Helga Lengenfelder
1983. XXX, 990 p. Bound DM 298.00
ISBN 3-598-20528-7, ISSN 0724-8717
(Handbook of International Documentation and Information, Vol. 17)

World Guide to Special Libraries covers about 32,000 special libraries in 159 countries. These are divided into 5 major subject categories with ca. 300 libraries in the general category – ca. 9,000 libraries in the fields of humanities – ca. 8,000 libraries specializing in social sciences – ca. 4,500 libraries specializing in medicine and life sciences – ca. 10,500 libraries covering science and technology. Each entry lists: address, telegram address, telephone and telex numbers, year of foundation, name of the director, important special holdings and collections, statistics on holdings, participation in the national loan system, membership in specialist confederations, participation in electronic information systems. A subject index with 271 entries provides access to all special libraries listed in the main part.

K·G·Saur München·New York·London·Paris
K·G·Saur Verlag KG · Postfach 711009 · 8000 München 71 · Tel. (089) 798901
K·G·Saur Inc. · 175 Fifth Avenue · New York, N.Y. 10010 · Tel. 212-9821302
K·G·Saur Ltd. · Shropshire House · 2-20 Capper Street · London WC1E 6JA · Tel. 01-637-1571
K·G·Saur, Editeur SARL. · 6, rue de la Sorbonne · 75005 Paris · Téléphone 354 4757

**Publishers' International Directory
with ISBN Index
Internationales Verlagsadressbuch
mit ISBN-Register**
11th Edition 1984
Managing Editor: Barbara Verrel
Editorial Staff: Marianne Albertshauser,
Astrid Kramuschka

1984. 2 vols. 1700 pages. Bound.
Subscription price through June 30,
1984 DM 348.00.
ISBN 3-598-20525-2
(Handbook of International Documentation and Information, Vol. 7)

The 11th edition of Publishers' International Directory, one of the most important and complete reference works for libraries and publishers alike, will be published in April 1984. This edition, brought up-to-date and once again expanded (with ca. 150,000 publisher entries, of which ca. 70,000 have ISBN prefixes), will appear in two volumes: Vol. I arranged alphabetically by country, and then alphabetically by firm name. Vol. II ISBN prefixes arranged numerically by area and publisher number. The fact that a modern data bank is updated daily and a short production time is made possible by the computer guarantees the most recent information. Thus, Publishers' International Directory is the most complete and actual directory of its type.

**International Books in Print
IBIP 1984**
English-language Titles
Published Outside the United States
and the United Kingdom
Edited by Archie Rugh

Part I: Author-Title List
1983. 2 Vols. 1,741 pages. Bound.
DM 448.00. ISBN 3-598-20583-X
Part II: Subject Guide
1983. 2 Vols. XXII,1449 pages. Bound.
DM 448.00. ISBN 3-598-20584-8
Complete edition: 4 Vols. 3190 pages.
DM 886.00. ISBN 3-598-20582-1

Published for the first time with a new Subject Guide, the third edition of this unique reference tool lists over 100,000 titles in English published outside the USA and the UK, covering both trade and non-trade publications. The new Subject Guide arranges the Author-Title list into three subject sequences: (1) 90 Dewey classes for main entries of non-fiction works; (2) an alphabetical country-by-country arrangement of fiction; (3) an index to persons as subjects.
The output of almost 3,000 publishers is included in IBIP's third edition, and in addition to including all the major European scholarly publishers, IBIP provides full bibliographic data and complete ordering information on thousands of current titles from little-known Third World publishers.

K·G·Saur München · New York · London · Paris

K·G·Saur Verlag KG · Postfach 71 10 09 · 8000 München 71 · Tel. (0 89) 79 89 01
K·G·Saur Inc. · 175 Fifth Avenue · New York, N.Y. 10010 · Tel. 212-9821302
K·G·Saur Ltd. · Shropshire House · 2-20 Capper Street · London WC1E 6JA · Tel. 01-637-1571
K·G·Saur, Editeur SARL. · 6, rue de la Sorbonne · 75005 Paris · Téléphone 354 47 57